Moses

Moses is revered as a great emancipator and lawgiver. The Ten Commandments and other laws that Moses received on Mount Sinai are an important component of modern legal codes in the United States and many other countries.

Money at its Best: Millionaires of the Bible

Abraham and Sarah
Daniel
David
Esther
Jacob
Job

Joseph
Moses
Noah
Samson
Solomon
Wealth in Biblical Times

MONEY
at its
BEST

Moses

Dorothy Kavanaugh

Mason Crest Publishers
Philadelphia

Produced by OTTN Publishing.
Cover design © 2009 TLC Graphics, www.TLCGraphics.com.

Mason Crest Publishers
370 Reed Road, Suite 302
Broomall PA 19008
www.masoncrest.com

Copyright © 2010 by Mason Crest Publishers. All rights reserved.
Printed and bound in the United States of America.

First printing

1 3 5 7 9 8 6 4 2

Library of Congress Cataloging-in-Publication Data

  Kavanaugh, Dorothy, 1969-
    Moses / Dorothy Kavanaugh.
      p. cm. — (Money at its best : millionaires of the Bible)
  ISBN 978-1-4222-0473-3 (hardcover)
  ISBN 978-1-4222-0848-9 (pbk.)
  1. Moses (Biblical leader) I. Title.
  BS580.M6K38 2008
  222'.1092—dc22
                                    2009015307

Publisher's Note: The Web sites listed in this book were active at the time of publication. The publisher is not responsible for Web sites that have changed their address or discontinued operation since the date of publication. The publisher reviews and updates the Web sites each time the book is reprinted.

Table of Contents

Moses and His Wealth	6
Introduction: Wealth and Faith	7
1. Moses the Millionaire	11
2. The Israelites in Egypt	18
3. The Birth and Early Life of Moses	38
4. Into the Wilderness	49
5. Message From a Burning Bush	59
6. Moses and Pharaoh	73
7. Miracle at the Red Sea	90
8. Hardship in the Desert	100
9. Leader of His People	118
Notes	130
Glossary	136
Further Reading	137
Internet Resources	138
Index	139
Illustration Credits	143
About the Author	144

Moses and His Wealth

- An an infant, Moses daily faced the threat of death. He was an Israelite boy, and the ruler of Egypt had decreed that all male Israelite infants should be killed. Desperate, his mother placed Moses in a basket and left it to float on the Nile River, trusting God that He would take care of her child. Then a miracle occurred—the pharaoh's daughter spotted the basket in the river, saw the infant inside, and felt sorry for him. She adopted the baby boy as her son. Moses's life changed in an instant—suddenly he was the grandson of the wealthiest and most powerful person in Egypt! As a result, Moses never wanted for anything when he was growing up.

- When Moses was sent to free the Israelites from their servitude in Egypt, God instructed him to have the Israelites plunder the Egyptians: "Every woman is to ask her neighbor and any woman living in her house for articles of silver and gold and for clothing, which you will put on your sons and daughters" (Exodus 3:22). This provided instant wealth for a people used to living in squalor and absolute poverty. God always provides for His people.

- Moses was truly blessed by the Lord. He was not only the leader of the people of Israel, but he was their judge and their spiritual leader as well. Deuteronomy 34:10-12 says, "No prophet has risen in Israel like Moses, whom the Lord knew face to face, who did all those miraculous signs and wonders the Lord sent him to do in Egypt—to Pharaoh and to all his officials and to his whole land. For no one has ever shown the mighty power or performed the awesome deeds that Moses did in the sight of all Israel."

- Many of the legends about Moses agree that he was extremely wealthy. The stories, however, disagree on the source of this wealth. Some say that he received his money through natural means, while other sources indicate that he gained his wealth through miracles. For example, according to one folktale, when God inscribed the Ten Commandments for Moses, the chips of stone that fell from the tablets turned into diamonds!

Introduction: Wealth and Faith

Many people believe strongly that great personal wealth is incompatible with deep religious belief—that like oil and water, the two cannot be mixed. Christians, in particular, often feel this way, recollecting Jesus Christ's own teachings on wealth. "Do not store up for yourselves treasures on earth, where moth and rust destroy, and where thieves break in and steal," Jesus cautions during the Sermon on the Mount (Matthew 6:19). In Luke 18:25, he declares, "It is easier for a camel to go through the eye of a needle than for a rich man to enter the kingdom of God"—a sentiment repeated elsewhere in the Gospels.

Yet in Judeo-Christian culture there is a long-standing tradition of material wealth as the manifestation of God's blessing. This tradition is amply reflected in the books of the Hebrew Bible (or as Christians know them, the Old Testament). Genesis 13:2 says that the patriarch Abram (Abraham) "had become very wealthy in livestock and in silver and gold"; the Bible makes it clear that this prosperity is a gift from God. Other figures whose lives are chronicled in

Genesis—including Isaac, Jacob, Joseph, Noah, and Job—are described as both wealthy and righteous. The book of Deuteronomy expresses God's promise of prosperity for those who obey his commandments:

> If you fully obey the Lord your God and carefully follow all his commands I give you today, the Lord your God will set you high above all the nations on earth. . . . The Lord will grant you abundant prosperity—in the fruit of your womb, the young of your livestock and the crops of your ground—in the land he swore to your forefathers to give you. (Deuteronomy 28:1, 11)

A key requirement for this prosperity, however, is that God's blessings must be used to help others. Deuteronomy 15:10–11 says, "Give generously . . . and do so without a grudging heart; then because of this the Lord your God will bless you in all your work and in everything you put your hand to." The book of Proverbs—written during the time of Solomon, one of history's wealthiest rulers—similarly presents wealth as a desirable blessing that can be obtained through hard work, wisdom, and following God's laws. Proverbs 14:31 promises, "The faithless will be fully repaid for their ways, and the good man rewarded for his."

Numerous stories and folktales show the generosity of the patriarchs. According to Jewish legend, Job owned an inn at a crossroads, where he allowed travelers to eat and drink at no cost. When they offered to pay, he instead told them about God, explaining that he was simply a steward of the wealth that God had given to him and urging them to worship God, obey God's commands, and receive their own blessings. A story about Abraham says that when he moved his flocks from one field to another, he would muzzle the animals so that they would not graze on a neighbor's property.

After the death of Solomon, however, the kingdom of Israel

was divided and the people fell away from the commandments God had mandated. The later writings of the prophets, who are attempting to correct misbehavior, specifically address unethical acts committed to gain wealth. "You trample on the poor," complained the prophet Amos. "You oppress the righteous and take bribes and you deprive the poor of justice in the courts" (Amos 5:11, 12). The prophet Isaiah insists, "Learn to do right! Seek justice, encourage the oppressed.... If you are willing and obedient, you will eat the best from the land; but if you resist and rebel, you will be devoured by the sword" (Isaiah 1:17, 19–20).

Viewed in this light, the teachings of Jesus take on new meaning. Jesus does not condemn wealth; he condemns those who would allow the pursuit of wealth to come ahead of the proper relationship with God: "No one can serve two masters. ... You cannot serve both God and money" (Matthew 6:24).

Today, nearly everyone living in the Western world could be considered materially wealthier than the people of the Bible, who had no running water or electricity, lived in tents, walked when traveling long distances, and wore clothing handmade from animal skins. But we also live in an age when tabloid newspapers and trashy television programs avidly follow the misadventures of spoiled and selfish millionaire athletes and entertainers. In the mainstream news outlets, it is common to read or hear reports of corporate greed and malfeasance, or of corrupt politicians enriching themselves at the expense of their constituents. Often, the responsibility of the wealthy to those members of the community who are not as successful seems to have been forgotten.

The purpose of the series MONEY AT ITS BEST: MILLIONAIRES OF THE BIBLE is to examine the lives of key figures from biblical history, showing how these people used their wealth or their powerful and privileged positions in order to make a difference in the lives of others.

Moses brings the tablets of the law down from Mount Sinai, as imagined by the Renaissance artist Guido Reni.

Moses the Millionaire

Most people do not think of Moses as a wealthy person—a millionaire, to use a modern expression. After all, most people's knowledge of Moses and the events of his life come from the Bible and the way its stories have been explained and interpreted by their parents, teachers, or religious leaders over the years. But because of Moses's importance, his life has been the subject of hundreds of legends and folktales, intended to round out the Biblical portrait of this ancient lawgiver.

Many of the legends about Moses agree that he was extremely wealthy. The stories, however, disagree on the source of this wealth. Some say that he received his money through natural means, while other sources indicate that he gained his wealth through miracles. For example, according to one folktale, when God inscribed the Ten Commandments for Moses, the chips of stone that fell from the tablets turned into diamonds!

Most religious leaders, whether Jewish or Christian, would agree that Moses's wealth is a relatively minor part of his story. It is more important, they note, that Moses was a virtuous man who answered God's call to lead the Israelites out of bondage in Egypt, and that he was responsible for transmitting God's laws, including the Ten Commandments, to the Israelites.

However, the story of Moses must also be considered in many other important ways. In particular, he is the epitome of a great leader—one who is driven by a higher purpose, while at the same time considerate of those he rules; one whose intent is not to enrich himself at the expense of others, but to help all of his people to prosper. In our modern time, when it is impossible to escape the tabloid exploits of spoiled, selfish millionaire athletes and entertainers, while news headlines are dominated by scandals involving corrupt businessmen and shady politicians, the example of Moses is certainly appealing.

A Relevant Leader Today

Moses is one of the most famous figures of history, a man who stood up to the most powerful earthly ruler of his time, the pharaoh of Egypt. Stories about Moses—his miraculous rescue from the Nile River when he was an infant, his defiance of pharaoh and the plagues that were visited upon Egypt, and the Israelite crossing of the Red Sea, for example—have been taught to young people, and studied in houses of worship, for thousands of years.

As the man who presented God's law to the people, and who tradition says wrote the Pentateuch (the first five books of the Hebrew Bible, also called by Jews the Torah), Moses is arguably the most important figure in the development of Judaism. Deuteronomy 34:10, 12 notes, "No prophet has risen in Israel like Moses, whom the Lord knew face to face. . . . For no one has ever shown the mighty power or performed the awesome deeds that Moses did in the sight of all Israel."

Louis Ginzberg, a great Jewish scholar of the early 20th century, agrees with this assessment. "Moses is regarded not only as the greatest religious guide of Israel, but also as its first national leader; he is 'the wisest of the wise, the father of the prophets,'" he noted in his seminal seven-volume work *Legends of the Jews*. "Hence his unique position in Jewish legend, neither Abraham, the friend of God, not Solomon, the wisest of all men, nor Elijah, the helper in time of need, can lay claim to such a position."

Judaism is not the only religion to revere Moses. He is mentioned in the New Testament gospels more often than any other Old Testament figure, and most Christians respect Moses as a symbol of God's law. Muslims, Mormons, and Bahá'ís consider Moses one of the greatest prophets, and interpret his life as preceding and introducing their own centrally important figures: the Prophet Muhammad, Jesus Christ, or the Bab).

Moses and the story of the Exodus resonate today in popular consciousness. He has been a symbol of the civil rights movement, famously invoked by Martin Luther King Jr. and other leaders. The metaphor of an ideal figure who will lead people to the "promised land" is regularly summoned in politics, in sports, in business, and in many other secular endeavors.

WAS MOSES A REAL PERSON?

Other than the Biblical record and the stories derived from it, there is no evidence that Moses ever existed. Some scholars believe the story of Moses is a largely fictionalized account—perhaps loosely based on some long-forgotten leader—written to explain the origins of the ancient kingdom of Israel and to glorify its deity, Yahweh, just as other cultures have their own origin fables.

No Egyptian inscription or artifact has yet been discovered that explicitly mentions Moses or corroborates the events of the Exodus period as they are recorded in the Bible. This is troubling, for the ancient Egyptians were practically obsessive in recording the details of their daily lives. Over the past two centuries, archaeologists have discovered harvest inventories, tax reports, letters written by kings and court officials, descriptions of children's games and women's beauty rituals, recipes for making beer and wine, thousand-year-long lists of rulers, detailed descriptions of religious observances and funeral preparations, military and political histories, and writings on numerous other topics, covering all aspects of Egyptian life. But with regard to the Exodus story, the archaeological record is silent.

The events described in Exodus—the plagues, the destruction of Egypt's army, and the escape of Egypt's large slave population—would have had a tremendous impact on Egyptian life. Egypt would have suffered a severe economic collapse, compounded by a struggle for power to fill the vacuum caused by the pharaoh's sudden death. These problems might have continued for a generation. It seems unlikely that Egyptian chroniclers would not have recorded some information about such events.

On the other hand, those scholars who believe Moses was a real person can counter that, given the nature of the events of Exodus, it is extremely unlikely that any Egyptian text mentioning them will ever be found. Egyptian scribes would have had no incentive to record a sequence of events that included the defeat of their ruler, humiliation of their nation, and the annihilation of their army. On the contrary, rulers of the ancient world tended

Ancient Spin Doctors

In the ancient world, it was common for rulers to erect elaborate monuments boasting of their accomplishments. Modern scholars have found that these rulers often either ignored their failures and defeats altogether, or attempted to "spin" them by making them appear to be glorious victories.

A famous example of this kind of spin occurred during the reign of Pharaoh Ramses II. Archaeologists discovered monuments alluding to a great victory that the pharaoh's army had won over the Hittites at Kadesh. (The Hittites controlled an empire that included much of modern-day Turkey and Syria.) Egyptologists could not understand why the pharaoh had not followed up this victory by expanding into Hittite lands, especially since the battle had occurred as part of a campaign to expand Egypt's hegemony over neighboring lands. The truth was revealed when Hittite monuments recording the battle were discovered. The Egyptians had actually been surprised and badly defeated by the Hittites in a major chariot battle; the defeat had halted Ramses II's plans to expand his empire.

There are numerous other examples of ancient rulers who only recorded their successes, and either ignored their failures or tried to paint them in a more favorable light. It is possible that the rulers of Egypt tried to cover up their humiliating defeat at the hands of the Israelites by attempting to erase it from their recorded history.

Image of Pharaoh Ramses II in his chariot at the battle of Kadesh, from his funerary temple in Luxor. Although Egyptian records that have survived indicate Ramses won a victory at Kadesh, other sources say that the battle was a devastating defeat for Egypt.

to ignore their failures and defeats, or attempted to "spin" them as though they had been glorious victories.

It also is extremely unlikely that original Israelite artifacts dating from Moses's time will ever be found. Moses is believed to have lived more than 3,500 years ago. The ancient Israelites were a nomadic people who preserved their stories and traditions orally, rather than in written form. Israelite records and stories do not begin to appear until around 900 B.C.E.—hundreds of years after Moses is believed to have lived.

In addition, there are details in the Exodus story that may indicate its truthfulness, at least on some level. For example, the name *Moses* comes from an Egyptian root; it makes sense etymologically although the name itself is uncommon. Many scholars believe this lends authenticity to the Biblical account. If some Israelite writer had made

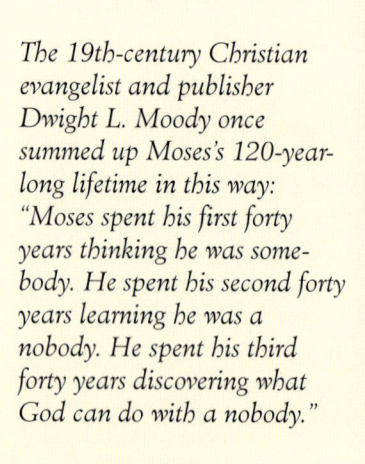

The 19th-century Christian evangelist and publisher Dwight L. Moody once summed up Moses's 120-year-long lifetime in this way: "Moses spent his first forty years thinking he was somebody. He spent his second forty years learning he was a nobody. He spent his third forty years discovering what God can do with a nobody."

up the story of Moses hundreds of years after it was supposed to have taken place, the writer probably would have given his (or her) protagonist an Israelite name or, if the scribe was familiar with Egyptian culture, he might have used a common Egyptian name.

Generally speaking, Exodus presents a story that is unlikely to have been conceived by a later writer creating a historical myth for his people. Why would the Israelites be interested in preserving and passing down a tradition in which they are slaves for hundreds of years, unless there is some core of truth to the story? "If you're making up history," notes Biblical scholar Richard Elliott Friedman, author of *Who Wrote the Bible*, "it's that you're descended from gods or kings, not from slaves." Friedman and other scholars cite other historical and documentary evidence that can be used to make a circumstantial case for a historical basis to the Exodus account—evidence that will be discussed in this book.

This biography will treat the Bible as its primary source, supplemented by archaeological findings and other writings related to Moses. For example, two Jewish historians of the first century C.E., Philo of Alexandria and Flavius Josephus, each wrote biographies of Moses as a way to introduce Judaism to residents of the Roman empire. Early Christian writers, including the Apostle Paul and the gospel author Luke, also wrote about Moses. And over the centuries Jewish rabbis and scholars recorded thousands of legends, called *midrashim*, in Hebrew texts that were meant to supplement and interpret the scriptures. Many of these stories offer fanciful, though interesting, stories related to the life of Moses. Finally, insights may be drawn from the works of contemporary scholars, both secular and religious, in an effort to present a true picture of Moses the millionaire.

2

THE ISRAELITES IN EGYPT

During the 19th century, some scholars believed they had found references in ancient Middle Eastern writings that supported the story of the Israelites being enslaved in Egypt. The term *Habiru* (sometimes rendered *Apiru* in English), which appears in a number of Egyptian and Mesopotamian letters and records, is very similar to the word *Hebrew*, which is used in the Biblical account to describe the descendants of Abraham who settled in Egypt. Two papyrus scrolls from the reign of Pharaoh Ramses II—who is believed by some scholars to have been the ruler of Egypt during the time of Moses—refer to a group of Habiru who were put to work moving stone for a temple. This, Bible scholars believed, was proof that the Hebrews had been forced to work as slaves in Egypt, just as the Biblical account said.

In the late 19th century, archaeologists uncovered an Egyptian royal archive, which contained more than 380 clay tablets, near the village of el-Amarna. The tablets, which proved to be from the reigns of several pharaohs, were written in the wedge-shaped characters of the Akkadian language, which was widely used for commerce and diplomacy in the ancient Middle East. Several of these cuneiform letters referred to the Habiru invading Canaan and conquering lands ruled by Egyptian vassals. For example, one Canaanite chieftain wrote to the pharaoh:

> The Apiru plunder all the lands of the king. If there are archers here in this year, the lands of the king, my lord, will remain intact; but if there are no archers here, the lands of the king, my lord, will be lost!

Initially, this discovery was believed to be evidence that the Biblical record was historically accurate. However, over time researchers determined that the term Habiru did not in fact refer to the Biblical Israelites, or any specific group of people for that matter. Instead, the word

This letter from a Babylonian ruler to Pharaoh Amenhotep IV, dating from around 1350 B.C.E., was found in the royal archive at el-Amarna. It is written in Mesopotamian Akkadian, the diplomatic language of the period.

Habiru was a common—and somewhat derogatory—term that could be loosely translated as "wanderer," "outsider," "fugitive," or "refugee," and was commonly used to refer to any group of people that lived outside the settled communities of the ancient world.

The people of Egypt certainly may have referred to the Israelites as Habiru. In fact, it's interesting to note that in the Bible, the term *Hebrews* typically appears when an Egyptian is involved in the conversation. In conversations between Moses and Yahweh, or involving the enslaved people, the term *Israelite* is used instead. Another similarity between the Habiru of antiquity and the Hebrews of the Bible is that both terms refer to groups of nomadic herdsmen. However, there is no way to connect the Hebrews of the Bible with the Habiru mentioned in Egyptian writings from the second millennium B.C.E.

Ancient Egyptians worshipped many deities. One of the most important figures in the Egyptian pantheon was Horus, pictured on this column. Horus was believed to have dominion over Egypt and the world of the living. Egyptians believed their pharaohs were the physical incarcation of Horus, and that they ruled Egypt on behalf of the god.

ANCIENT SUPERPOWER

Four thousand years ago, Egypt possessed one of the most advanced civilizations on earth. Egypt dominated the Eastern Mediterranean region both militarily and economically, and was a center of arts and culture. The ancient kingdom of Egypt was essentially confined to the Nile River valley and delta, where annual flooding produced a relatively narrow strip of fertile land, surrounded on all sides by arid North African desert.

Without regular flooding, which deposited rich alluvial soil washed from Central Africa along the Nile's banks, agriculture would have been impossible in Egypt. Even today in some parts of the land rain is so rare that it is considered a miracle when it occurs. The region around the modern capital, Cairo, receives on average less than two inches (5 cm) of rain annually, and some parts of Egypt can go years without receiving any measurable rainfall at all. Recognizing the importance of the river to sustaining this region's civilization, the Greek historian Herodotus famously referred to Egypt as "the gift of the Nile."

Although in general the flooding of the Nile was an annual event, it was not entirely predictable. The extent of the flooding could vary from year to year. Some years, major floods would destroy irrigation dams and wash away the mud-brick homes of the Egyptians. Other years, the river would not rise. When this happened, famine and starvation resulted.

Famine was not unusual in ancient Egypt. At times the river would not flood for several years in succession, leading to significant distress. This is known to have occurred during the rule of the Pharaoh Zoser (circa 2650 B.C.E.), who is known for building the famous step-pyramid. An inscription on a monument near the First Cataract of the Nile, created about 1,000 years later, claims to be a copy of a document from Zoser's time. It reveals the pharaoh's despair about a serious and lengthy famine in Egypt:

> I was in distress on the Great Throne, and was in affliction of heart because of a very great evil, for in my time the Nile has not overflowed for a period of seven years. There was scarcely any grain; fruits were dried up; and everything which they eat was short. Every man robbed his neighbor....

It was a seven-year period of famine like the one described in this inscription that, according to the Bible, brought the Israelites to Egypt in the first place, more than 400 years before the birth of Moses. That history is recorded in Genesis, the first book of the Torah and Bible.

ORIGINS OF THE ISRAELITES

According to the Genesis account, the Israelites are descended from a man named Abraham, who was born in a Mesopotamian city called Ur of the Chaldees around 2200 B.C.E. Abraham is sometimes called the first monotheist, a person who worships only one deity. This is technically not accurate—Abraham is better described as a henotheist, someone who worships one god while acknowledging that other gods exist and can exert influence on the world. According to the Bible, however, Abraham worships only God. In return God promises Abraham certain things: that he will have many descendants, that they will one day possess the land of Canaan, and that through Abraham's descendants the world will be blessed.

In Genesis, this promise, or covenant, takes the form of a solemn and binding legal agreement between two parties. "I will make you very fruitful; I will make nations of you, and kings will come from you," God tells Abraham.

The Israelites in Egypt

"The whole land of Canaan, where you are now an alien, I will give as an everlasting possession to you and your descendants after you; and I will be their God" (Genesis 17:6, 8).

But these things will not happen overnight, God warns Abraham. Instead, his descendants will undergo a long period of testing before they can possess Canaan:

> Then the Lord said to [Abraham]: "Know for certain that your descendants will be strangers in a country not their own, and they will be enslaved and mistreated four hundred years. But I will punish the nation they serve as slaves, and afterward they will come out with great possessions" (Genesis 15:13–14).

The Israelites are descended from Abraham's grandson, Jacob, who is given the name Israel after an

Moses's ancestor Abraham obeyed God, even when He demanded that Abraham sacrifice his son Isaac. Because of Abraham's faith and his willingness to follow God's commands, God permitted Abraham to sacrifice a ram in Isaac's place. This 1645 painting is by the Dutch master Rembrandt.

encounter described in Genesis 32:22–32. In this story, Jacob wrestles with an angel and refuses to let him go even after being seriously injured. In the morning, the angel blesses Jacob, calling him Israel, which, the Bible explains, means "he struggles with God."

Jacob/Israel and his family are nomadic herdsmen, caring for flocks of sheep and goats. They are constantly on the move, seeking good pastureland. They eventually settle in Canaan, sharing the land with many other tribal groups, today known collectively as the Canaanites.

DIVINE INTERVENTION

The sequence of events that leads to the arrival in Egypt of the Israelites—as Jacob's descendants will one day be called—is an unusual one that is told in the final half of the book of Genesis. In the Bible, Jacob is the father of twelve sons. However, he favors his eleventh son, Joseph, which makes the others very jealous. Joseph doesn't help matters when, as a young man, he tells his brothers about a dream in which he is set above them, and they bow down to him. Annoyed, his ten older brothers consider killing Joseph, but at the last minute they decide to sell him as a slave to a trading caravan taking spices and other goods from Gilead, a territory in Canaan, south to Egypt. (To explain his disappearance, the older brothers dip Joseph's robe in the blood of a slaughtered goat, and tell their father that a wild animal has killed Joseph.)

Although Jacob grieves for the son he believed to be dead, Joseph prospers in Egypt, with God's help. Joseph is sold to a high-ranking government official, and becomes his most trusted servant. Eventually, Joseph comes to the attention of the pharaoh, who has had an unsettling dream and cannot find anyone in Egypt who can interpret its meaning. God gives Joseph the correct meaning of pharaoh's dream, enabling him to predict the future: there will be seven years of plentiful harvest in Egypt, followed by seven years of devastating famine. Joseph then suggests to the pharaoh a system of gathering and storing grain during the seven good years, in order to mitigate the impact of the famine years. The pharaoh is impressed with Joseph; he places him in charge of this project and makes him the second most powerful man in Egypt, after only the pharaoh himself. Genesis records:

> Joseph stored up huge quantities of grain, like the sand of the sea; it was so much that he stopped keeping records because it was beyond measure.... The seven years of abundance in Egypt came to an end, and the seven years of famine began, just as Joseph had said. There was famine in all other lands, but in the whole land of Egypt there was food. . . . And all the countries came to Egypt to buy grain from Joseph, because the famine was so severe in all the world. (Genesis 41:49, 53–54, 57).

In Canaan, Jacob's family is starving because of the famine, so Joseph invites them to settle in Egypt, where there is plenty of food. Joseph forgives his brothers for selling him into slavery, now recognizing the hardships he suffered as part of God's plan to ensure the survival of Abraham's descendants. He tells his brothers, "You intended to harm me, but God intended it for good to accomplish what is now being done, the saving of many lives. So then, don't be afraid" (Genesis 50:20–21).

STRANGERS IN A STRANGE LAND

The Bible lists 70 members of Jacob's family who made the trip to Egypt at Joseph's request. This must have been a frightening prospect—giving up their homes in Canaan,

Members of a Semitic tribe—distinguished by the colorful stripes on their robes—ask permission to enter Egypt. Detail from a mural found in a pharaoh's tomb, circa 1850 B.C.E.

the land that God had promised them, for an unknown future in a strange place—but God assures Jacob that he is making the right decision. "Do not fear to go down to Egypt, for I will make of you a great nation there," God tells the patriarch. "I will go down with you to Egypt, and I will also surely bring you up again" (Genesis 46:3–4).

Jacob and the members of his family had good reason to be fearful about traveling to Egypt. Ancient Egypt was a cosmopolitan center of learning and culture, and its people felt a strong antipathy toward nomadic sheep and goat herders like the members of Jacob's clan. This bias was so strong that Joseph warned his brothers before they arrived in Egypt, "every shepherd is an abomination to the

Egyptians" (Genesis 46:34). Joseph encourages his brothers to downplay the fact that they are shepherds; instead, Joseph suggests that they tell pharaoh only that they are seeking pasture for their livestock, without being specific. Perhaps Joseph hoped that the pharaoh would assume his family tended herds of cattle, which the ancient Egyptians considered sacred animals.

In a famous commentary on the book of Exodus, the 19th-century Old Testament translators and scholars Carl Friedrich Keil and Franz Delitzsch noted that the negative attitude toward herdsmen who wandered the ancient Middle East with their flocks of sheep and goats was reflected in Egyptian writings and monuments that are 3,000 to 4,000 years old:

> The dislike of the Egyptians to shepherds arose from the fact that the more completely the foundations of Egypt rested upon agriculture, the more did the Egyptians associate the idea of rudeness and barbarism with the very name of a shepherd. This is . . . attested in various ways by the monuments on which shepherds are constantly depicted as lanky and withered, distorted, emaciated, and sometimes almost ghostly figures.

However, despite Egyptians' poor view of nomads, the pharaoh welcomes Jacob's family, telling Joseph, "The land of Egypt is before you; settle your father and your brothers in the best part of the land. Let them live in Goshen. And if you know of any among them with special ability, put them in charge of my own livestock" (Genesis 47:6).

The pharaoh's positive response may simply indicate his appreciation for Joseph's performance in managing the famine. However, many scholars believe there could be another reason that the pharaoh was not troubled by the arrival of a band of despised shepherds. Perhaps the pharaoh was not actually Egyptian!

Sometime around the year 1,750 B.C.E., a nomadic tribe from Central Asia began migrating into Egypt. Scholars are uncertain whether this people, known as the Hyksos, actually invaded and conquered Egypt, or simply moved into the land of a long period of time and eventually found themselves able to seize power from the pharaohs. It is certain, however, that Hyksos kings ruled much of Egypt for more than a hundred years, from about 1648 to 1540 B.C.E.

Historically, the word *Hyksos* has often been translated "shepherd kings," leading many 19th and 20th century scholars to speculate that a Hyksos pharaoh would not have shared the traditional Egyptian aversion to herdsmen. In recent years, however, scholars have determined that "foreign rulers" is a more accurate translation of *Hyksos* than "shepherd kings." Still, it is worthwhile to note that as something of an outsider himself, a Hyksos ruler probably would have been more willing than an Egyptian ruler to appoint a foreigner like Joseph to a position of power within the government.

A Community Grows in Egypt

Goshen, where the Hebrews settled, is believed to have been located east of the Nile delta. This region has long been considered excellent pastureland. "Bedouin have kept their flocks in that general area throughout history," notes Charles F. Pfeiffer in *Old Testament History*. "Even today, Arab Bedouin regularly appear in the Wadi Tumilat area between Lake Timsah and the Delta. The pasture land is covered with clumps of bulrushes, papyrus, and shrubs."

The Israelites flourished in Goshen along with their livestock. The Bible describes the rapid growth of the

Israelite community in Goshen a number of times. "Now the Israelites settled in Egypt in the region of Goshen," notes Genesis 47:27. "They acquired property there and were fruitful and increased greatly in number." During the next four centuries, the population of Israelites continued to expand. Exodus 1:6–7 explains, "And Joseph died, all his brothers, and all that generation. But the children of Israel were fruitful and increased abundantly, multiplied and grew exceedingly mighty; and the land was filled with them."

At some point, however, an event occurred that led to a major change for the Israelites. The Bible relates that a new pharaoh came to power, one "who did not know Joseph" (Exodus 1:8). In the traditional reading of this passage, the new ruler didn't know about or respect the accomplishments of Joseph, and therefore didn't understand why the immigrant Israelites had good lands and privileged positions. However, it is also possible to read this verse as reflecting a historical shift of power in ancient Egypt—the end of Hyksos rule and the establishment of the Eighteenth Dynasty by the Egyptian Pharaoh Ahmose I during the mid-16th century B.C.E.

DATING THE EVENTS OF EXODUS

A problem in relating the story of Moses is that it is impossible to date events with certainty. Although the Bible mentions several different pharaohs in the Book of Exodus, it never provides specific names for any of these rulers. In addition, no evidence exists outside the Bible to corroborate the major events of Exodus—the departure of a large group of Israelite slaves from Egypt or the miraculous destruction of the pharaoh's army in the sea.

Over the centuries, Christians have developed various systems in an attempt to date Old Testament events. One of the most ambitious of these was *Annales veteris testamenti, a prima mundi origine deducti* ("Annals of the Old Testament, deduced from the first origins of the world"), a history created by the Anglican archbishop of Ireland, the Reverend James Ussher, in 1650. Ussher used genealogies of Adam, Noah, Abraham, and other legendary figures mentioned in the Bible, along with other dates given in the scriptures, to determine that the world had been created in 4004 B.C.E. He dated the events of Exodus to 1491 B.C.E.

By the late 19th century, the discovery of fossils and the emergence of the Theory of Evolution caused many people to reject Ussher's date for creation. But while some Bible scholars agreed that the extensive genealogies listed in Genesis could not be used to determine the age of the Earth, they continued trying to date various Biblical events, linking them to archaeological discoveries in Egypt, Palestine, and Persia during the 19th and 20th centuries.

Today, many Evangelical Christians believe that Moses led the Israelites out of Egypt around 1446 B.C.E. This date has been derived from other dates and accounts given in the Bible—in particular, working backward from a chronology of rulers listed in the First Book of Kings. For secular scholars, however, this date is problematic. Thutmose III, pharaoh from 1479 to 1425 B.C.E., is considered one of Egypt's greatest military leaders. During his long reign, his armies captured more than 300 cities, expanding his rule from Africa to Mesopotamia. There is plenty of historical evidence about his rule, and no evidence that suggests his army was destroyed, or that Egypt was devastated by plagues during his rule.

Another pharaoh who has traditionally been linked to the events of Exodus is Ramses II (sometimes spelled

This statue—believed to represent the Egyptian pharaoh Ramses II—is located at the Great Temple of Ramses in southern Egypt. A popular tradition holds that Ramses was the pharaoh who kept the Israelites in slavery; however, the true identity of the pharaoh mentioned in the Bible may never be known.

Ramesses II), who reigned from 1279 to 1213 B.C.E.; in the fourth century C.E. the early Christian historian Eusebius of Caesarea identified Ramses as the pharaoh of the oppression. Egyptian records discovered more recently have been used to support this claim. For example, one document from this pharaoh's reign contains a report of efforts to supply grain to a group of workers quarrying stone for a monument. Some scholars believe the hieroglyphics used in the document to identify the workers refer specifically to the Hebrews.

Ramses II is probably the last Egyptian ruler who could have been pharaoh when the Israelites were living in Goshen. A 10-foot-tall stele attributed to his son and successor Merneptah, who ruled from 1213 to 1203 B.C.E., records Merneptah's various military exploits, including Egyptian victories over several city-states in Canaan. One inscription on the stele reads, "Canaan is captive with all woe. Ashkelon is conquered, Gezer seized, Yanoam made nonexistent; Israel is wasted, bare of seed." The mention of Israel on this stele indicates that the Israelites were established in Canaan by around 1208.

The question of which pharaoh ruled during Moses's time is controversial, and no ruler can be definitively shown to be correct. Other candidates include Ahmose I (1550–1525 B.C.E.), Amenhotep II (1427–1401 B.C.E.), and Amenhotep IV (also known as Akhenaton, 1352–1336 B.C.E.) Some writers—including the first century Jewish historian Flavius Josephus—have speculated that the Israelite departure from Egypt coincided with the Hyksos expulsion.

It seems likely, however, that the events of Exodus occurred during the period that followed Hyksos rule, known as the New Kingdom. This period included three Egyptian dynasties: the Eighteenth (1550–1292 B.C.E.), Nineteenth (1291–1191), and Twentieth (1190–1077). The word *pharaoh* was first used to describe the ruler of Egypt during the Eighteenth Dynasty. It also seems logical that the Israelites would have suffered at the hands of the Egyptians after the Hyksos were forced from power.

A Matter of National Security

It is not hard to understand why an Egyptian ruler—no matter who it was—would have become nervous about the large number of Israelites living in his domain. The period of Hyksos domination would have concerned many people long after these foreigners were expelled. Modern archaeologists have found that Egyptian rulers of the Eighteenth Dynasty tried to erase any trace of Hyksos rule, destroying or defacing their monuments. This can be read as a sign that Egyptian nationalism reemerged during this period. That nationalism, combined with the natural suspicion of Egyptians toward outsiders, spelled trouble for the Israelites.

Part of the problem was that the Israelite population had grown rapidly over the four centuries that the people had lived in Goshen. The Bible says that the Israelites "were fruitful and multiplied greatly and became exceedingly numerous, so that the land was filled with them (Exodus 1:7).

In the pharaoh's point of view, controlling this growing Israelite population was a matter of national security. The threat that the Israelites might assist a foreign invader against the Egyptian rulers presented a serious limitation on their power. This clearly occurred to the pharaoh mentioned in Exodus, who told his advisors, "Come, let us deal shrewdly with them, lest they multiply, and it happen, in the event of war, that they also join our enemies and fight against us" (Exodus 1:10).

The pharaoh's plan did not involve driving the Israelites out of Egypt. Instead, the Egyptians opted to enslave the Israelites, intending to reduce the population by working the people to death in the service of the state. The Israelites were put to work building storehouses for grain in Pithom and Ramesses, two major Egyptian cities near the Goshen region. (The latter became capital of Egypt when Pharaoh Ramses II ruled the land.) In addition, the Septuagint—a Greek translation of the Hebrew scriptures that was completed between the third and first centuries B.C.E.—indicates that the enslaved Israelites worked on projects at On (later Heliopolis), a major city near the Nile delta that in ancient Egypt was the center of worship for the sun god, Ra.

The Bible says, "[The Egyptians] made their lives bitter with hard labor in brick and mortar and with all kinds of work in the fields; in all their hard labor the Egyptians used them ruthlessly" (Exodus 1:14). The Jewish historian Philo of Alexandria, writing in the first century C.E., adds more details about the effect of the pharaoh's plan, writing that the Israelites worked

> day and night without interruption, having no rest or respite, and not even being allowed time so much as to sleep . . . so that in a short time their bodies failed them, their souls having already fainted beneath their afflictions.
>
> And so they died, one after another, as if smitten by a pestilential destruction, and then their taskmasters threw their bodies away unburied beyond the borders of the land, not suffering their kinsmen or their friends to sprinkle even a little dust on their corpses, nor to weep over those who had thus miserably perished.

GENOCIDE IN EGYPT

The pharaoh hoped that the hard labor, as well as forced separation of workmen from their wives, would check the growth of the Israelite population. This certainly was the cause in a more recent implementation of a similar plan, carried out by the leaders of Nazi Germany during the 1930s and 1940s; the Holocaust nearly eliminated Jews from Europe, resulting in the deaths of almost 6 million people. But despite the efforts of the pharaoh's overseers, the Bible reports that this plan had no impact: "But the more they afflicted them, the more they multiplied and grew. And [the Egyptians] were in dread of the children of Israel" (Exodus 1:12). A related story, or midrash, says that God purposely increased the fertility of the Israelites in order to frustrate the plans of the pharaoh, who was trying to thwart God's own plan to make the Israelites a great nation.

The Israelites in Egypt 35

מָה שֶׁנֶּאֱמַר וַיָּשִׂימוּ עָלָיו
שָׂרֵי מִסִּים לְמַעַן עַנֹּתוֹ
בְּסִבְלֹתָם וַיִּבֶן עָרֵי מִסְכְּנוֹת
לְפַרְעֹה אֶת פִּתֹם וְאֶת
רַעַמְסֵס

וַיִּתְּנוּ

This illustration from a haggadah, a Jewish text read during the Passover seder, shows the Hebrews building cities for the Egyptian pharaoh. This haggadah was created in northern Spain around 1350 C.E.

Next, the pharaoh attempts to enlist midwives in his population control scheme, telling them to kill the newly born sons of the Israelites. However, the midwives refuse to take part in the murder of children—the Bible says they "feared God and did not do as the king of Egypt commanded them, but saved the male children alive" (Exodus 1:17). When they are called before the angry pharaoh and asked why, the midwives come up with an excuse: "Because the Hebrew women are not like the Egyptian women; for they are lively and give birth before the midwives come to them." Whether or not the pharaoh buys this excuse is unknown, although the Bible indicates that the midwives not only survive this encounter with the ruler, they subsequently prosper because they have done the right thing.

Pharaoh then turns to a new plan, decreeing that all male children of the Israelites must be cast into the Nile River. This campaign to murder Israelite babies may be the first recorded incidence of a state-sponsored genocide.

According to popular tradition, the enslaved Israelites provided the labor to build some of Egypt's greatest monuments, including several of the pyramids.

In essence, Egyptians are told that it is their civic duty to find and kill baby Israelite boys.

The Bible account does not give any specific details about the way these murders were carried out, but Jewish rabbis writing thousands of years later invented plenty of gory examples. According to one midrash, each Israelite slave was ordered to make a certain number of bricks each day; if he failed, his youngest child would be mortared into the wall instead of the bricks. Another story describes how the Egyptian death squads found hidden babies: they took an Egyptian mother and her young child into the Israelite home they were searching, then pinched the Egyptian infant hard enough to make it cry. This would cause a hidden Israelite baby to cry as well, enabling the Egyptian soldiers to find the concealed child. Once discovered, the soldiers would fulfill pharaoh's command and dispatch the child: "When they discovered one, they tore him from his mother's breast by force, and thrust him into the river."

The scriptures say, "The Israelites groaned in their slavery and cried out, and their cry for help because of their slavery went up to God. God heard their groaning and he remembered his covenant with Abraham, with Isaac and with Jacob. So God looked on the Israelites and was concerned about them" (Exodus 2:23–25). He would soon send someone who would deliver His people from the power of the Egyptian pharaoh.

The Birth and Early Life of Moses

No more than a few years after the pharaoh decreed that every male Israelite child should be thrown into the Nile River, an Israelite couple named Amram and Jochebed give birth to a son described in the Bible as a "beautiful child" (Exodus 2:2). For three months, Jochebed hides the baby from the Egyptian death squads who are roaming Goshen. Throughout this time she must have been constantly terrified that at any minute someone passing her home would hear the infant's wail, break in, and rip the infant from her arms.

A Desperate Plan

Finally, recognizing that she can no longer keep up this deception, Jochebed comes up with a desperate plan to save her son. She constructs a small basket out of bulrushes, weaving a cover to keep the sun out of her child's face. Then Jochebed coats this basket with oily resin to make it watertight,

The Birth and Early Life of Moses 39

places her child inside, and sets it adrift along the edge of the Nile River, where it floats among the reeds along the riverbank. The Bible reports that Jochebed's daughter—later identified as Miriam—hides on the riverbank, watching to see what will happen to her baby brother.

Soon, the pharaoh's daughter comes down to the river to bathe, accompanied by a number of young female servants. When pharaoh's daughter spots the floating basket, she directs one of her maids to retrieve it. When the cover is pulled off, the bright sun causes the infant to wail. The Egyptian princess might be expected to dump the floating basket over into the river, silencing the infant's cry forever. Instead, however, the pharaoh's daughter feels sympathy for the baby and decides to save him.

To the casual reader, Jochebed's effort to save her son by setting him adrift in the river may not seem like much of a plan. The basket could easily have capsized and sunk, floated away, or been discovered and purposely dumped over. However, there may be more to the story than is explicitly recorded in the Bible. Some commentators have speculated that Jochebed might have tied up the raft so that it would not float away; this would enable her to sneak down to the river and feed the child at different times during the day without risking exposure in her home. Alternately, Jochebed may have observed the pharaoh's daughter bathing in the river, perhaps on numerous occasions, and noticed something about the young princess that indicated she would feel empathy and pity for an abandoned Hebrew infant, rather than fulfilling her father's order that baby Hebrew boys be drowned.

In any case, as the pharaoh's daughter holds the crying infant in her arms on the banks of the river, Miriam steps out of her hiding place and asks, "Shall I go and call a nurse for you from the Hebrew women, that she may nurse the child for you?" (Exodus 2:60). Pharaoh's daughter responds to this offer affirmatively, so Miriam runs back to her home and returns with her own mother. When Jochebed arrives, pharaoh's daughter promises to pay her to nurse the child.

According to Jewish folklore, a Hebrew wet nurse was required because the infant Moses refused to suckle at the breast of an Egyptian woman recruited for this same purpose. Whether or not this story is true, it is a fact that the practice of hiring a wet nurse, particularly among royalty, was common in the ancient world. Archaeologists have discovered clay cuneiform tablets that contain contracts between adoptive mothers and professional wet nurses, recording in detail the rights and duties of each party.

WHAT'S IN A NAME?

Because no one can say for certain which pharaoh was the ruler in Moses's time, it is impossible to know the name of the Egyptian woman who adopts the infant found in the river. In his book *Jewish Antiquities* (ca. 94 C.E.), Flavius Josephus calls the pharaoh's daughter Thermuthis, while the fourth century Christian writer Eusebius recorded a tradition that her name was Merris in his apologetic work *Praeparatio Evangelica* ("Preparation for the Gospel"). According to the later writings of Jewish rabbis, the name of the pharaoh's daughter was Bityah, Bithia, or Batya.

And although the infant she rescued would become known to history as Moses, it is similarly uncertain exactly what his Israelite parents called him. According to one midrash, Amram named the boy Tobia, which means "God is good." However, other Jewish legends and stories give other names to the infant, including Heber ("reunited") and Jekuthiel ("because I set my hope upon God, and he gave him back to me").

The Birth and Early Life of Moses 41

The infant Moses is drawn from the waters of the Nile by the women attending pharaoh's daughter.

The name *Moses* is of Egyptian origin, probably based on the word *mes* or *mesu*, which means "one born of" or "a child of." This was commonly used in Egyptian names—for example, the name *Thutmose* means "born of Thoth," and may indicate that this pharaoh was born on a feast day sacred to this ancient Egyptian deity. The Hebrew version of the name, *Mosheh*, is a play on words—specifically the Hebrew word *masheh*, meaning "to draw out," a reference to pharaoh's daughter drawing the infant out of the river. The familiar name Moses, used in most English-language editions of the Bible, is a translation of Mosheh from the Septuagint version of the Jewish scriptures.

WEALTHY AND PRIVILEGED

The Bible does not provide any information about Moses's childhood. However, as the adopted grandson of the pharaoh he would have enjoyed a wealthy and privileged upbringing. The pharaoh and his family were exceedingly rich—Egyptians considered pharaoh a god, and technically he owned all the land and livestock of Egypt. Farmers paid the pharaoh an annual tax in exchange for the use of their land or livestock, and Egyptians were also required to spend part of each year working on monuments and public works for the pharaoh. It is safe to say that Moses never went hungry or suffered as a child; he probably had an array of servants to care for him and perform daily tasks.

According to folktales retold by Louis Ginzberg, when Moses is still an infant pharaoh's daughter brings him to her father's court, declaring that Moses is her son and will one day succeed her father as ruler of Egypt: "I have brought up a child who is divine in form and of an excellent mind, and as I received him through the bounty of the river in a wonderful way, I have thought it proper to adopt him as my son and as the heir of thy kingdom."

In another story, two-year-old Moses is dining with the pharaoh when he becomes attracted to the king's glittering crown. He playfully reaches up and removes it from the king's head, placing it on his own. Pharaoh's advisors are horrified at this bad omen; they warn the ruler that this is a sign indicating that this child will one day take the government of Egypt into his own hands. Moses must be killed, they argue, before he becomes a threat.

However, according to this tale the pharaoh is reluctant to execute his grandson. While his advisors discuss what should be done, the Angel Gabriel intervenes in the guise of an old man. He argues that the boy is innocent, and sets up a test.

> If it please the king, let him place an onyx stone before the child, and a coal of fire, and if he stretches out his hand and grasps the onyx stone, then shall we know that the child hath done with wisdom all that he hath done, and we will slay him. But if he stretches out his hand and grasps the coal of fire, then shall we know that it was not with consciousness that he did the thing, and he shall live.

When the test begins Moses, guided secretly by the angel, grasps the hot coals, thus burning his hand but saving his life. The infant cries out in pain and attempts to

Moses and Sargon

The story of the infant Moses in the bulrushes is in some ways very similar to a Mesopotamian legend about a famous ruler named Sargon. According to the legend, Sargon's mother, a priestess, places her infant in a basket made from reeds and sets it afloat on the Euphrates River. A man named Akki, who works on the river, finds the infant and adopts him. Sargon eventually grows up to become a mighty general; he conquers an enormous empire in Mesopotamia and established the Akkadian dynasty around the year 2360 B.C.E.

However, there are important differences in the two stories as well. Sargon's mother wants to rid herself of an unwanted child, while Moses's mother is seeking to protect her son. In addition, Moses does not grow up to be a tyrant like Sargon; instead, he is a prophet who delivers the Israelites from the power of another tyrant, the pharaoh of Egypt.

This 17th-century painting by the Dutch master Jan Lievens the Elder depicts a moment in the Jewish folktale in which Moses knocks off the pharaoh's crown.

cool his scorched hand by placing it in his mouth. However, a few burning embers remain on his hand, burning Moses's tongue and mouth. The rabbis used this tale to explain Exodus 4:10, a Bible passage in which Moses tells God that he is not a good speaker. "For all of his life, he became slow of speech and of a slow tongue," explains Louis Ginzberg.

By passing the test, Moses was permitted to continue his privileged life as a member of pharaoh's family, and it seems he was educated and trained for a high position in the court. The historian Josephus wrote that the pharaoh had no son, so Moses was groomed to become his heir.

THE EDUCATION OF A PRINCE

In the New Testament book Acts of the Apostles, a speech by the early Christian teacher and martyr Stephen indicates that Moses was highly educated. Acts 7:22 says,

"Moses was educated in all the learning of the Egyptians." The Bible does not give details about this learning, but archaeological research and other writings can be used to help fill in the blanks.

People of the ancient Middle East recognized Egypt as a great center of learning. Egypt was more advanced culturally than the city-states of neighboring Canaan or even of Mesopotamia. Much of Moses's education would have taken place in Egyptian temples, as these were the major repositories of knowledge in ancient times. Records, royal decrees, and other information were stored in temples and could be accessed by the priests.

Moses may have gone to school at a city called On (later known as Heliopolis, because it was the center of worship for the Egyptian sun god, Ra). This city was near the Nile delta, just two days travel from the former capital of Egypt, Memphis. In the third century B.C.E. an Egyptian historian named Manetho claimed that Moses had been trained as a religious leader at Heliopolis. However, Manetho himself was a priest of the sun god, so this claim may be of dubious veracity.

If he was trained as a priest, Moses would first have learned the intricacies of reading and writing hieroglyphs, the ancient Egyptian picture-writing system used for religious purposes by the priests and scribes. To be fluent, an Egyptian would have to learn more than 2,000 hieroglyphs. Moses would also have learned how to read Akkadian, a Mesopotamian language made using pointed sticks to make wedge-shaped marks in wet clay, which was later dried to preserve messages and keep accounts. Akkadian was the common language of international diplomacy during Egypt's New Kingdom period, and most of the messages between Egyptian rulers and the kings of the Canaanite or Mesopotamian city-states were written in this ancient cuneiform language. Moses would also have studied the sciences, medicine, astronomy, theology, philosophy, and the law.

When Moses was in school, he may have had classmates from any number of number of Canaanite and Mesopotamian communities. As archaeologist and historian Charles Pfeiffer explains in *Old Testament History*:

> The Egyptian school system was a highly developed one. Sons of tributary princes from the Syro-Palestinian city states were sent to Egypt to study with Egyptian royalty. In this way they became pro-Egyptian in politics, and when a throne was vacant, the rulers of Egypt sought to place one of these Egyptian-trained vassals in the position of power. The boys also served as hostages, for the king of a city-state would hardly attack an Egyptian garrison if he thought his own son might suffer as a result.

From these students, Moses would have learned something about the geography, history, and culture of peoples living beyond Egypt's borders—knowledge that would become useful later in his life. Moses would also have heard the story of Sinuhe, a legendary member of the Egyptian court who left his home and spent years wandering through Canaan and other foreign lands.

One folktale says that the pharaoh's daughter took great care to educate Moses, hiring teachers from foreign lands to come to Egypt and tutor her son. She spared no expense to have him instructed, and Moses was more than equal to the challenge. "By reason of his admirable endowments of mind, he soon excelled his teachers in knowledge," noted the author of this tale. "His learning seemed a process of mere recollecting, and when there was a difference of opinion among scholars, he selected the correct one instinctively, for his mind refused to store up anything that was false."

A Stoic Warrior?

It is clear that young Moses was a formidable young man. The Bible describes him as "mighty in words and deeds" (Acts 7:22). Philo of Alexandria wrote that Moses mastered numerous disciplines, from mathematics to music to philosophy. Philo also described Moses as a man able to suppress the passions of youth:

> And he tamed, and appeased, and brought under due command every one of the other passions which are naturally . . . violent and unmanageable. . . . [I]n short, he repressed all of the principal impulses and most violent affections of the soul, and kept guard over them as over a restive horse, fearing lest they migh tbreak all bounds and get beyond the power of reason which ought to be their guide to restrain them, and so throw everything everywhere into confusion.

This characterization doesn't really match the Biblical portrait of Moses; in fact, while Moses was still a young man he would give in to passion and commit an act that would permanently change the direction of his life. Rather than being rooted in some truth, Philo's passage seems to be informed by Stoic philosophy, which taught that emotions were destructive and that self-control was the way to true happiness. Although he was Jewish, Philo believed strongly in Stoic teachings and often incorporated them into his writings.

Another depiction of the young Moses that doesn't necessarily mesh with the Biblical description of the older man is Josephus's assertion that he was a skilled soldier and military tactician. In *Jewish Antiquities*, he describes an invasion of Egypt by an army from neighboring Ethiopia. Oracles tell the pharaoh that Moses is the only man who can stop the invaders. Moses takes command of the Egyptian army and, according to Josephus, skillfully leads his men to gain surprise: "He came upon the Ethiopians before they expected him; and, joining battle against them, he beat them and deprived them of the hopes they had of success against the Egyptians, and went on to overthrow their cities, and indeed made a great slaughter of these Ethiopians."

According to this tale, Moses leads the Egyptian army into Ethiopia, where he besieges and sacks the city of Saba. This victory is made possible by assistance from the daughter of the city's ruler, who "happened to see Moses as he led the army near the walls, and fought with great courage," and subsequently fell in love with him. She lets the Egyptians into the city, and they conquer. After thanking God for this triumph Moses marries the Ethiopian woman, then returns to Egypt.

The Bible does not mention that Moses has military experience, or that he has an Ethiopian wife. Still, this may have been the incident that the early Christian Stephen was referring to when he described Moses as "mighty in words and deeds." The writings of Irenaeus and other early Christians indicate that they were also familiar with Josephus's story, and did not reject it out of hand.

In any case, the point of such stories about Moses is to paint him as a remarkable young man: a learned scholar who was brave and of strong character. The Bible and the related tales show that, from a young age, Moses was clearly destined for greatness. However, he had no idea that his fortunes were about to change dramatically.

4

INTO THE WILDERNESS

By the time he is about 40 years old, Moses is a wealthy, powerful, and respected man in Egyptian society. Somewhere along the line, however, he has learned the truth about his ancestry—that the pharaoh's daughter was not his real mother, and that he is descended from the despised, enslaved Israelites. His parents Jochebed and Amram were Levites, members of the tribe of Israel that traditionally served as priests or religious leaders. It is possible that, somehow, one of them communicated this knowledge to the prince of Egypt.

In a sermon on the life of Moses delivered during the fourth century, the Christian bishop Gregory of Nyssa (335–394 C.E.) indicated that as an adult Moses completely renounced Egyptian culture and society. "After he had left childhood and had been educated in pagan learning during his royal upbringing, he did not choose the things considered glorious by the pagans," writes St. Gregory. "Nor did he any longer recognize as his mother that wise woman by whom he had been adopted, but he returned to his natural mother and attached himself to his own kinsmen."

WATCHING THE HEBREWS

The Bible does not explain how Moses learned of his ancestry. It simply states, "One day, after Moses had grown up, he went out to where his own people were and watched them at their hard labor" (Exodus 2:11).

It is not clear from the Biblical account whether this is the first time Moses has watched the Israelites working. Jewish legends about Moses indicate that this was a regular behavior, and that he tried to make things easier on the Israelites when he could. According to one midrash, Moses is so upset at the oppression of the Israelites that one day he decides to lend a hand at the worksite. "He dismissed all thought of his high station at court, shouldered a share of the burdens put upon the Israelites, and toiled in their place," goes this tale, as recorded in *Legends of the Jews*. "The result was that he not only gave relief to the heavily laden workmen, but he also gained the favor of Pharaoh, who believed that Moses was taking part in the labor in order to promote the execution of the royal order."

In another tale, Moses goes to the pharaoh and requests that the Hebrew slaves be given a day off from work. "It is an admitted fact," said Moses, "that if a slave is not afforded rest at least one day in the week, he will die of overexertion. Thy Hebrew slaves will surely perish, unless thou accordest them a day of cessation from work." Of course, according to the Bible and other midrash, this outcome—working the slaves to death—is exactly what pharaoh intended. So it seems unlikely that this story—in which the pharaoh agrees to Moses's request and allowed the Hebrews to rest one day each week—is true.

Murder in the Desert

During the visit recorded in the Bible, however, Moses observes a violent scene: "He saw an Egyptian beating a Hebrew, one of his own people" (Exodus 2:11). Moses becomes very angry and lashes out—an incident that contradicts Philo's assertion that he has mastered his emotions. Looking around to make sure that no one is watching, he strikes down and kills the Egyptian overseer, rescuing the Israelite slave from his beating. Moses then tries to hide his crime by burying the slain Egyptian in the desert.

Moses kills the overseer, as described in Exodus 2. Another Biblical perspective on this killing appears in the New Testament scripture Acts of the Apostles, which reports, "And when [Moses] saw one of them being unjustly treated, he defended him and took vengeance for the oppressed by striking down the Egyptian. And he supposed that his brethren understood that God was granting them deliverance through him, but they did not understand" (Acts 7:24–25).

Some contemporary writers have speculated that Moses was trying to stir up a slave rebellion that would enable him to take power in Egypt, and thus rescue the Israelites from their affliction. The writings of Flavius

Josephus tend to agree with this theory, although Josephus's book does not mention Moses's murder of the Egyptian. Instead, Josephus wrote that after the successful Ethiopian military campaign, the pharaoh and his advisors feared that Moses would "take occasion, from his good success, to raise a rebellion."

Again, this theory reflects an aspect of Moses's character that contradicts other depictions. Only an ambitious young man—and one who was supremely confident in his own ability—would attempt to seize power in this way. The Biblical account does not present Moses as being particularly ambitious, and various folktales and legends, as well as the writings of Philo and others, typically show Moses as a wise young man who was not interested in personal gain, and whose attention was always focused on helping others.

Forced to Flee

If Moses really is trying to stir up a rebellion among the Hebrew slaves and thinks they will rally behind his leadership to overthrow the pharaoh, he is sorely mistaken. When Moses returns to the worksite the next day, he finds several Israelites arguing. When he attempts to intervene in their quarrel, he is rebuffed. "Who made you ruler and judge over us," asks one angry Israelite, who then tauntingly reveals that he knows all about Moses's murderous rage of the previous day: "Are you going to kill me, as you killed the Egyptian?" (Exodus 2:14).

Confusion and fear would likely have been Moses's response to this revelation. If his act of murder becomes known, he will be ruined. And in fact the Bible reports that pharaoh has learned about the murder, and has decided to arrest and execute the renegade prince of Egypt. Moses's only option is to flee, leaving behind the wealth and privilege he has known and starting over in a wild desert land with nothing.

Eluding the Egyptian authorities sent to arrest him, Moses travels across the Red Sea and through the Sinai Desert, taking difficult paths so that he would not be followed. "[B]ecause the public roads were watched, he took his flight through the deserts, and where his enemies could not suspect he would travel; and though he was destitute of food, he went on, and despised that difficulty courageously," wrote Josephus. The Bible says that Moses eventually arrived in a distant land called Midian, where he would be safe from the pharaoh.

Arrival in Midian

Midian is the name of an area east of the Gulf of Aqaba; the territory stretched over parts of the present-day states of Jordan and northwestern Saudi Arabia. According to the Bible, this region was named for a son of the ancient patriarch Abraham, who had settled there centuries earlier. The Midianites were nomadic herdsmen, who wandered the region with their sheep and goats looking for pastureland. The Midianites also traded gold, spices, and slaves between the Arabian Peninsula and Egypt; in fact, hundreds of years earlier Joseph had been sold by his brothers to a Midianite slave caravan, which had taken him to Egypt. The Midianites were polytheists, but their main deity was named Baal-Peor. (Baal was the name commonly given to the most powerful of the fertility or nature gods worshipped by the various Canaanite or Phoneician tribes.)

When Moses arrives in Midian, possessing nothing, he stops at a well. While there he notices seven young women starting to draw water for their father's flocks. A group of jealous shepherds arrive. Worried that if they have to wait

Moses defends the Midianite sisters, as described in Exodus 2:17: "Some shepherds came along and drove [the women] away, but Moses got up and came to their rescue and watered their flock."

for these women to finish their chores, there will not be enough water for their own livestock, the shepherds chase away the young women and their sheep.

There seems to be something in Moses's character that will not enable him to stand by while others are being mistreated. Moses intervenes—just as he did when he saw the Israelite slave being beaten by his Egyptian overseer. In another indication of his personal bravery, the disgraced prince of Egypt drives the shepherds away from the well.

A New Family

The young women turn out to be daughters of Jethro, the high priest of Midian. (The Bible also calls the man Reuel and, in the book of Judges, Hobab.) When they return home, their father asks how the animals had been watered so quickly. "An Egyptian delivered us out of the hand of the shepherds," the daughters replied, "and moreover he drew water for us and watered the flock" (Exodus 2:19).

Jethro tells his daughters to go back and fetch Moses, and bring him to their home. They comply, and when the younger man arrives Jethro takes a liking to him. Eventually, he invites Moses to marry his daughter, Zipporah. Moses agrees, and begins taking care of his father-in-law's livestock.

In his *De Vita Moysis* ("Life of Moses"), the fourth-century bishop Gregory of Nyssa describes Jethro as "a man with insight into what is noble and perceptive in judging the habits and lives of men." According to Gregory, Jethro

> saw in one act—the attack on the shepherds—the virtue of [Moses], how he fought on behalf of the right without looking for personal gain. Considering the right valuable in itself, Moses punished the wrong done by the shepherds, although they had done nothing against him. Honoring the young man Moses for these acts and judging his virtue in his manifest poverty more valuable than great riches, the man gave him his daughter in marriage and, in keeping with his authority, he permitted Moses to live as he wished. Moses lived alone in the mountains away from all the turmoil of the marketplace; there in the wilderness he cared for his sheep.

So Moses has gone from being one of the most powerful and respected men in Egypt to being a simple herdsman in a desert backwater. If Moses truly were an ambitious man, it seems unlikely that he would have accepted this dead-end job. Josephus, however, presents the position in a different light—as one of responsibility: "[Reuel] appointed him to be the guardian and superintendent over his cattle; for of old, all the wealth of the barbarians was in those cattle."

The Shepherd as Ruler

In the Bible, the shepherd often serves as a metaphor for a king or a great leader. David, the greatest of Israel's later kings, was a shepherd boy when he slew the Philistine giant Goliath. In the Bible, David asserts his ability to defeat his enemy by telling the Israelite King Saul, "Your servant has been keeping his father's sheep. When a lion or a bear came and carried off a sheep from the flock, I went after it, struck it, and rescued the sheep from its mouth. When it turned on me, I seized it by its hair, struck it and killed it. . . . The Lord who delivered me from the paw of the lion and the paw of the bear will deliver me from the hand of this Philistine" (1 Samuel 17:34–37). In the tenth chapter of the New Testament Gospel of John, Jesus describes himself as the "good shepherd" who never leaves even a single sheep in danger.

The rabbinical authors of the Talmud and Midrash agreed that working as a shepherd could make someone a better leader. "By the way [Moses] tended the sheep, God saw his fitness to be the shepherd of His people, for God never gives an exalted office to a man until He has tested him in little things," wrote Louis Ginzberg in *Legends of the Jews*, "Thus Moses and David were tried as shepherds of flocks, and only after they had proved their ability as such, He gave them dominion over men."

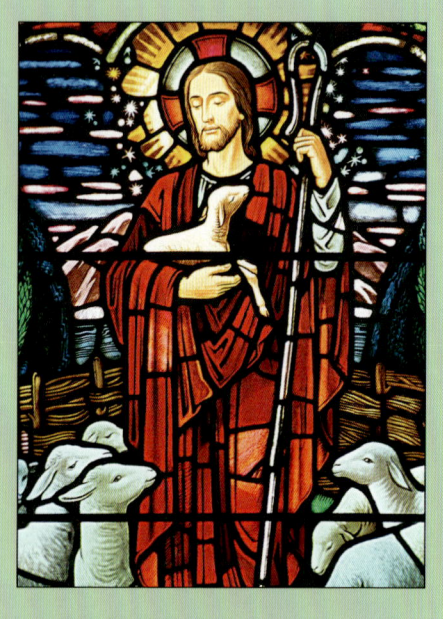

Philo wrote, "Moses took his father-in-law's herds and tended them . . . to qualify him for becoming the leader of a people, for the business of a shepherd is a preparation for the office of a king to any one who is destined to preside over that most manageable of all flocks, mankind."

Into the Wilderness

At the very least, Midian is a place where Moses will be safe from pharaoh's vengeance. Moses and Zipporah soon have a son, whom he names Gershom. This name reflects Moses's new refugee status. According to Exodus 2:21, it means "I have become an alien in a foreign land."

MOSES THE SHEPHERD

Life as a shepherd in the dusty, dry land of Midian would have been nothing like the life Moses had been accustomed to as a pampered prince in the lush country of Egypt. In the ancient world, a shepherd's life was dirty and dangerous. Every day, the shepherd had to find food and water for his flock and protect the animals from lions, jackals, hawks, and other predators. It was a lonely life;

Moses in the house of Jethro. Detail from a Byzantine mosaic, circa 800 C.E.

the shepherd had no help, and the flock relied solely on his ability to survive. The shepherd had to make tough decisions, sometimes sacrificing a sick or injured animal for the good of the flock.

The midrashim depict Moses as watching over the flock with loving care. According to one story, he tracks down a young sheep that has wandered away from the flock and returns it safely. Another story indicates that as a shepherd Moses shows respect for other peoples' property. He would take care to pasture his sheep in an open meadow, rather than a field that belonged to someone else. "Jethro had no reason to be dissatisfied with the services rendered to him by his son-in-law," the story notes. "During the forty years Moses acted as his shepherd not one sheep was attacked by wild beasts, and the herds multiplied to an incredible degree."

According to the Biblical account, Moses was forty years old when he arrived in Midian, and he tends Jethro's flocks for the next forty years. Of course, it seems unlikely to the modern reader that an eighty-year-old man would still be able to handle the hard outdoor life of a shepherd, with its daily requirement of physical exertion. In addition, the expression "forty years" is a fairly common one in the bible—for example, later in Exodus, the Israelites will wander for forty years in the wilderness, and in the book of Judges there are several peaceful periods that last for forty years. Many modern scholars believe that this term is simply an expression that dates to the time before Bible stories were written down. Some believe that "forty years" refers to a generation (i.e., about 18 to 20 years); others think it is simply a kind of oral storytelling shorthand meaning "a long time."

Message from a Burning Bush

One day, while pasturing his flock on the side of Mount Horeb, Moses encounters a strange sight: a bush that appeared to be on fire, but is not consumed by the flames. "I will go over and see this strange sight—why the bush does not burn up," Moses decides (Exodus 3:3).

The actual location of Mount Horeb is uncertain, although tradition places it in the southeastern Sinai Peninsula, a 6,500-foot (1,981 meter) peak known today as Ras es-Safsaf. In the Bible, Mount Horeb is described as "the mountain of God." It may have been a place that the Midianites considered sacred, although that raises the question of what Moses was doing there with his sheep in the first place. Alternately, it may have gained that name and reputation because of the encounter that follows.

As Moses walks over to the strange bush, he hears a voice calling his name:

"Moses! Moses!" The shepherd responds, "Here I am." Then the voice calls out, "Do not come any closer. Take off your sandals, for the place where you are standing is holy ground." The voice continues, explaining: "I am the God of your father, the God of Abraham, the God of Isaac, and the God of Jacob." (Exodus 3:4–6). Moses, stunned by this divine revelation, kicks off his sandals and falls on his face, afraid to look at the burning bush. (Throughout the book of Exodus, smoke and fire are used to symbolize the divine presence.)

Next, God explains why he is appearing to Moses at this time and in this place:

> I have indeed seen the misery of my people in Egypt. I have heard them crying out because of their slave drivers, and I am concerned about their suffering. So I have come down to rescue them from the hand of the Egyptians and to bring them up out of that land into a good and spacious land, a land flowing with milk and honey—the home of the Canaanites, Hittites, Amorites, Perizzites, Hivites and Jebusites. And now the cry of the Israelites has reached me, and I have seen the way the Egyptians are oppressing them. So now, go. I am sending you to Pharaoh to bring my people the Israelites out of Egypt (Exodus 3:7–10).

THE NAME OF GOD

Moses is awed and surprised to be in the God's presence. The Israelites probably told stories about their God and his promises to Abraham, and his conversations with Isaac, Jacob, and the other patriarchs. Moses may or may not have been familiar with these tales—the Bible doesn't say—but Moses does immediately recognize God as a powerful deity. However, God has not been heard from in

Message From a Burning Bush

some time—more than 400 years, in fact, during which time the Israelites had been enslaved by Egypt—and Moses is, understandably, reluctant to embrace this strange duty. "Who am I," he asks, "that I should go to Pharaoh and bring the Israelites out of Egypt?" Next, he stalls for time. "Suppose I go to the Israelites and say to them, 'The God of your fathers has sent me to you,' and they ask me, 'What is his name?' Then what shall I tell them?" (Exodus 3:12–13)

God's reply, "I Am Who I Am," (translated into English as Yahweh; see "The Name of God," page 62) expresses what Jews (and later, Christians) would recognize as the most important elements of God's character: dependability and faithfulness. Unlike the various names for God used earlier in the Bible (such as El Elyon, meaning "God Most High," or El Shaddai, "God Almighty"), I Am Who I Am indicates that God is not limited to any particular characteristic—He is what He is. Furthermore, this name indicates the unchanging nature of God: He was worshipped by Abraham hundreds of years before Moses was born, and will still be the same

God speaks to Moses from the burning bush. Detail from an illuminated French manuscript of the 15th century.

long after the death of Moses. "This is my name forever," God tells Moses, "the name by which I am to be remembered from generation to generation" (Exodus 3:14–15)

The Name of God

During the time that the Jewish people were exiled to Babylon (586 to 539 B.C.E.), it became the accepted practice not to pronounce the name of God. Instead, in scriptural texts—many of which were first written down during the Babylonian captivity—the name of God was represented by four Hebrew consonants (YHWH). These four unpronounceable letters are known as the tetragrammaton. In ancient manuscripts, Jewish scribes included notes with the name indicating to readers that the word "Adonai" ("My Lord") should be read rather than the name of God.

Beginning in the 13th century, a small number of Christian scholars began trying to translate the tetragrammaton into Latin, Greek, and other languages. Because these monks and scribes did not consult Jewish experts, they made the mistake of combining the four consonants of the tetragrammaton with the vowels in "Adonai." As a result the name of God was translated *Iehouah*, which later evolved into Jehovah. (In the Latin alphabet, "J" and "U" originally represented vowel variants of the consonants "I" and "V." "J" and "U" did not emerge as separate letters until the 1700s.)

Christians used the name Jehovah until the 19th century, when a German scholar named Wilhelm Gesenius (1786-1842) suggested that the tetragrammaton could be more properly translated YHWH, or in English, Yahweh. Gesenius based this proposal on his translation of ancient Greek and Hebrew texts, as well as on grammar conventions of Semitic languages like Hebrew and Aramaic.

Today, most Biblical scholars accept Yahweh as the most accurate transliteration of the tetragrammaton, although Jehovah and other forms also continue to be used by some Christian groups.

With the name question cleared up, God gives Moses additional instructions:

> Go, assemble the elders of Israel and say to them, "The Lord, the God of your fathers—the God of Abraham, Isaac, and Jacob—appeared to me and said: I have watched over you and have seen what has been done to you in Egypt. And I have promised to bring you up out of your misery in Egypt into . . . a land flowing with milk and honey."
>
> The elders of Israel will listen to you. Then you and the elders are to go to the king of Egypt and say to him, "The Lord, the God of the Hebrews, has met with us. Let us take a three-day journey into the desert to offer sacrifices to the Lord our God. But I know that the king of Egypt will not let you go unless a mighty hand compels him. So I will stretch our my hand and strike the Egyptians with all the wonders that I will perform among them. After that, he will let you go (Exodus 3:16–20).

Not only does God promise that he will free the Israelites, he adds that they will profit greatly from His encounter with Egypt. "I will make the Egyptians favorably disposed toward this people, so that when you leave you will not go empty-handed," God tells Moses. "Every woman is to ask her neighbor and any woman living in her house for articles of silver and gold and for clothing, which you will put on your sons and daughters. And so you will plunder the Egyptians" (Exodus 3:21–22).

Moses's Miracles

These promises seem unbelievable to Moses. Perhaps at this moment he thinks back forty years earlier, when he had failed in his attempt to unite the Israelites under his leadership and deliver them from slavery. At that time the

Israelites had refused to follow Moses even though he was a wealthy and powerful member of Egyptian royalty. If he returns to Egypt now, a shepherd emerging from the desert without any visible source of authority, only an unexpected commission from a legendary and unknown God, the Israelites will probably laugh at or ignore him. How, he asks God, can he convince the Israelites to listen to him?

God responds by giving Moses the power to perform several miraculous signs, which will show that he has in fact been sent by a powerful deity. First, Moses is able to turn his shepherd's staff into a snake. This sign would have undoubtedly had a strong impact on people living in ancient Egypt; the snake was a symbol of sovereignty, and cobras made of gold or other metals were worn on the front of the pharaohs' headdresses to indicate their authority as rulers.

For the second sign, Moses is able to cause a skin disease; he is also given power to cure this disease. In the Bible, the Hebrew word for this malady is often translated inaccurately as "leprosy." However, the Biblical description of the disease does not resemble leprosy, and the original translation in this form resulted from confusion when the original Hebrew text was translated into Greek. The disease Moses is able to cause and cure therefore may be another skin disease, such as psoriasis, impetigo, or eczema, which have symptoms that more closely resemble the Biblical description.

The third sign is more gruesome. "If they do not believe these two signs or listen to you, take some water from the Nile and pour it on the dry ground," God says. "The water you take from the river will become blood on the ground" (Exodus 3:9). Unlike the first two signs, which God actually shows Moses how to perform, Moses must accept on faith that he will be able to perform this third wonder when the appropriate time comes.

A Reluctant Messenger

Moses remains reluctant, and tries to tell God that he is not a suitable messenger. He urges God to send someone else. "Oh Lord, I have never been eloquent, neither in the past nor since you have spoken to your servant," he says. "I am slow of speech and tongue" (Exodus 4:10). At one time, Biblical interpreters believed this meant Moses had a speech impediment, and this concept became part of the popular image of Moses. Stories like the Jewish folktale about how Moses burned his tongue as an infant were attempts to explain the history of this speech impediment. However, most modern commentators on the Bible believe that this passage indicated simply that Moses felt he was not quick-witted enough to contend with the pharaoh and the learned members of his court, rather than that he had a lisp or some other speech defect.

God has a ready answer: "Who gave man his mouth? Who makes him deaf or mute? Who gives him sight or makes him blind? Is it not I, the Lord? Now go; I will help you speak and will teach you what to say" (Exodus 4:12).

At this point in the narrative, Moses is getting desperate. His excuses haven't worked, so he finally resorts to a direct approach. "O Lord, please send someone else to do it," he asks (Exodus 4:13).

Elsewhere in the Old Testament, God is described as being "slow to anger" (Exodus 34:6, Nehemiah 9:17, Psalms 103:8 and 145:8, and Jonah 4:2, to name a few references). Now, however, his patience with Moses has run out, and he is tired of the excuses. In a way, God gives in to Moses's request—but not in the manner that the elderly shepherd had intended. The scripture says:

> Then the Lord's anger burned against Moses, and he said, "What about your brother, Aaron the Levite? I know he can speak well. He is already on his way to meet you, and his heart will be glad when he sees you. You shall speak to him and put words in his mouth; I will help both of you speak and will teach you what to do. He will speak to the people for you, and it will be as if he were your mouth and as if you were God to him. But take this staff in your hand so you can perform miraculous signs with it (Exodus 4:14–17).

Thus God does grant Moses's request—send someone else—but at the same time does not release Moses from the obligation that He has placed on him—to go to Egypt and deliver the Israelites from slavery. Aaron will join Moses and help him in this mission.

THE BROTHER OF MOSES

This is the first time in the scripture that readers learn that Moses has a brother. Jewish tradition states that Aaron is the oldest son of Amram and Jochebed, and that he is three years older than Moses. He may therefore have been one of the male children born with the connivance of the Hebrew midwives, who refused to kill the baby boys despite pharaoh's command, and he must have been born before the king issued his order to drown all male Hebrew infants in the Nile. Aaron apparently is younger than his sister Miriam, who watched over infant Moses while his reed basket bobbed in the water along the riverbank.

According to the *Jewish Encyclopedia*, "While Moses was receiving his education at the Egyptian court and during his exile among the Midianites, Aaron and his sister remained with their kinsmen in the eastern border-land of Egypt. Here he gained a name for eloquent and persuasive speech." Like his parents, Aaron was a Levite, a member of the priestly class of Israel. Tradition says that he was already a respected religious leader in the Israelite community; his influence would make it easier for the people to accept Moses as a deliverer sent from God.

Thus out of excuses—and perhaps afraid to anger God any further by continuing to resist—Moses agrees to return to Egypt on what will become his life's defining work. First he visits his father-in-law Jethro, and asks for his permission to return to Egypt. When Jethro agrees, "Moses took his wife and sons, put them on a donkey and started back to Egypt. And he took the staff of God in his hand" (Exodus 4:20).

A Strange Encounter

The passage above (Exodus 4:20) is the first time Moses's second son is mentioned; later in Exodus the son's name is revealed to be Eliezar. Although the Bible does not give details about when this boy was born, it is possible that he was an infant when Moses and Zipporah set out on their journey. That might help to explain one of the strangest passages in the Bible, Exodus 4:24–26, which says:

> At a lodging place on the way, the Lord met Moses and was about to kill him. But Zipporah took a flint knife, cut off her son's foreskin and touched Moses' feet with it. "Surely you are a bridegroom of blood to me," she said. So the Lord let him alone.

Moses has finally agreed to obey God, and is on his way to Egypt, so why would God want to kill him? Christian exegetes typically interpret the incident as an indication that Moses is still reluctant to commit himself fully to God's mission. God has assured Moses that He will deliver the Israelites out of Egypt because of His covenant with Abraham. However, Moses had failed to circumcise his own son, as that covenant required.

"What did all this mean?" asks the evangelical Christian preacher Charles Swindoll in his book *Moses: A Man of Selfless Dedication*. Taking the traditional line, he explains, "It meant Moses had overlooked a part of the covenant that demonstrated obedience to God. Every godly Jew was to circumcise the male child; he was to see to it that this was done properly and without exception. Moses would have known that well. Gentiles were known as the uncircumcised ones. But Jews? This was a physical mark of their obedience before God, who planned and designed the procedure. In this unique demonstration, a man said to God, 'My family, my heart, and my home are dedicated to You and set apart for You, O God of Israel.'"

The requirement of circumcision is detailed in Genesis 17:9, 11–12, 14: "Then God said to Abraham, 'As for you, you must keep my covenant, you and your descendants after you for the generations to come. . . . Every male among you shall be circumcised. You are to undergo circumcision, and it will be the sign of the covenant between me and you. For the generations to come every male among you who is eight days old must be circumcised, including those born in your household or bought with money from a foreigner. . . My covenant in your flesh is to be an everlasting covenant. Any uncircumcised male, who has not been circumcised in the flesh, will be cut off from his people; he has broken my covenant.'"

However, this standard explanation is flawed in several ways. Because Moses was educated as an Egyptian, it seems plausible that he may not in fact have understood the connection between circumcision and Abraham's covenant. Unlike modern believers, Moses did not have a

Book of Genesis to guide him; the stories in that book were passed down orally among Abraham's descendants, and would not be written down until, at the earliest, the time of Moses—and more likely hundreds of years after Moses's death.

Additionally, although many people today believe circumcision set the Israelites apart from other people, the truth is that circumcision was not uncommon in the ancient Near East. The removal of the foreskin from the male penis was usually done as part of a manhood ritual around the time of puberty.

Detail from a painting in the Sistine Chapel in Rome showing the circumcision of Moses's younger son during the journey to Egypt. Religious scholars disagree on the events that occur in Exodus 4:24–26.

"The fact that it was often regarded as a preparation for marriage may be inferred from the fact that the Semitic word for bridegroom (*hathen*) literally means 'circumcised,' and the corresponding word for father-in-law (*hothen*), literally means 'he who circumcises,'" notes archaeologist Charles Pfeiffer. "Among the neighbors of Israel who practiced circumcision in ancient times were the Edomites, Ammonites, Moabites, and Egyptians."

The archaeological record is supported by the Biblical account, as circumcision among non-Israelites is noted in several books, including Jeremiah and Ezekiel. For example, Jeremiah 9:25–26 notes, "'The days are coming,' declares the Lord, 'when I will punish all who are circumcised only in the flesh—Egypt, Judah, Edom, Ammon, Moab and all who live in the desert in distant places. For all these nations are really uncircumcised, and even the whole house of Israel is uncircumcised in heart.'"

Some rabbinical sources believe that the Midianites—who like the Israelites were descended from one of Abraham's sons—may have understood the importance of circumcision and continued to perform the ritual while the enslaved Israelites, laboring for centuries in Egypt, neglected the practice.

In its discussion of the incident, another midrash provides the following explanation: "The reason why their son had remained uncircumcised until then was that Jethro had made the condition, when he consented to the marriage of his daughter with Moses, that the first son of their union should be brought up as a Gentile."

Finally, going back to the original Hebrew texts, it is not clear exactly who is being circumcised. Pronouns are used without identifying whether they refer to Moses, Yahweh, or the son of Moses and Zipporah. Christian commentators typically note that it was the older son, Gershom, while some rabbinical sources indicate it was their younger son, Eliezer (who is not mentioned by name until much later in the Exodus story). If this son were an infant when Moses and Zipporah set out, it is possible that the incident at the lodging place on the way occurred on the eighth day after his birth. This would therefore comply with God's deadline for infant circumcision.

A few contemporary Bible experts believe that perhaps it was Moses himself who was not circumcised, and that Zipporah performed the ritual on him, rather than on their son. These experts contend that at some point the original text was edited to read "her son's foreskin" rather than

"Moses's foreskin." If their analysis is accurate, it would help explain Zipporah's "bridegroom of blood" comment.

Poor editing could also explain the problem of Yahweh's sudden and deadly anger toward Moses. In the previous passage, God had spoken with Moses, calmly giving him final instructions on what he was to do once he reached Egypt. Then, with Moses attempting to do what he was told, God is suddenly ready to kill him. Contemporary scholars believe that the beginning of this section of Exodus may originally have contained additional verses; these would have explained more clearly the reasons for God's anger.

MOSES CONTINUES TO EGYPT

After this harrowing ordeal, Moses and Zipporah apparently decide to part ways temporarily. The Bible does not explicitly say that they separate, but Zipporah and the children are not mentioned again until much later in the story—after Moses has led the Israelites out of Egypt. That passage, in Exodus 18:2–5, indicates that she returned to her father's house in Midian until she received word from Moses that he had succeeded in his mission, then she came out to meet him in the Sinai desert with their sons. Perhaps after the near-fatal encounter with God, Moses feels—with good reason—that his life is in danger, and wants to send his family away for their protection.

As for Moses, he continues on his way toward Egypt. At the same time his brother Aaron receives a message from God that Moses is coming. Their meeting is briefly discussed in the Bible; Aaron believes Moses's story and agrees to assist him when he goes to speak with the pharaoh.

Aaron then brings Moses before the leading Israelites—the elders of the community—and relates the tale that Moses has told him. Apparently the elders are a little more skeptical than Aaron. The Bible relates that Moses "also performed the signs before the people, and the believed" (Exodus 4:30–31), which indicates that they did not take Moses and Aaron seriously at first. But after more than 400 years of hard slavery, once the Israelites see Moses's miraculous signs they must have felt that a great opportunity for deliverance was at hand.

Moses himself may have felt confident as he and Aaron prepared for an audience with the pharaoh. After all his grandfather, who had sought to kill him, was now dead and a new pharaoh had taken his place. Moses would soon learn, however, that this Egyptian king is not as susceptible to signs and wonders as the Israelites had been.

MOSES AND PHARAOH

The events of Moses's life probably took place during the New Kingdom period, which lasted from the 16th to the 11th century B.C.E. Because the identity of the pharaoh that Moses and Aaron met is unknown, it is impossible to say where their meeting took place. Ancient Egypt had several capital cities, including Memphis, Thebes, and, during the rule of Ramses II, Pi-Ramesses—a city specifically mentioned the Bible as a place where the Israelites worked on construction projects.

One thing that is certain is that the pharaoh would have considered himself a divine being, and would have been regarded as such by his subordinates. Pharaohs were considered the living incarnation of the god Horus, son of Osiris (the Egyptian god of life, death, and fertility) and Isis (goddess of wisdom and protection). According to Egyptian mythology, Osiris was a good ruler who was killed by his evil brother Seth, who seized the throne. Isis rescued and preserved her slain husband's body, and when Horus grew older he defeated Seth and avenged his father's death. Through his magic Horus brought Osiris back to life, so that he could rule over the world of the dead, while Horus ruled over the land of the living through his physical incarnations, the pharaohs.

As a divine being, therefore, pharaoh's response to the request by Moses and Aaron is predictable: "Who is the Lord, that I should obey him and let Israel go? I do not know the Lord and I will not let Israel go" (Exodus 5:2). When Moses and Aaron persist, pharaoh angrily asks, "Why are you taking the people away from their labor? Get back to your work!" After dismissing the troublemakers, pharaoh issues a new order to his slave drivers and worksite foremen:

> You are no longer to supply the people with straw for making bricks; let them go and gather their own straw. But require them to make the same number of bricks as before; don't reduce the quota. They are lazy; that is why they are crying out, "Let us go and sacrifice to our God." Make the work harder for the men so that they keep working and pay no attention to lies (Exodus 5:4, 7–9).

Pharaoh's response seems excessive. Moses did not ask pharaoh to free the Israelites, only to let them go a short distance away to worship their god. According to several sources, a three-day journey into the wilderness for the Israelite community, which included women and children, would be the equivalent of a one-day march for the Egyptian army, so the Israelites could not have used the trip to escape from pharaoh's grasp.

On the other hand, pharaoh may have been suspicious simply because the Hebrews have never previously men-

Moses and Aaron speak to the Egyptian pharaoh, asking him to allow the Israelite slaves to go into the desert and worship Yahweh. The Egyptian word pharaoh *was originally used to refer to the palace where the king of Egypt lived. It was not until the reign of Amenhotep IV (ca. 1353–1336* B.C.E.*) that the word was used to describe the Egyptian ruler.*

tioned needing to sacrifice to a god in the wilderness. And there is another element of his response that is worth considering. The pharaoh probably grew up with Moses—he may even have been a stepbrother or a close relative—and would have known Moses from the days when he was the royal favorite. The expression "familiarity breeds contempt" was surely as true 3,500 years ago as it is today. The pharaoh may also have remembered the incident in which Moses killed an Egyptian foreman in an apparent attempt to rile up the Hebrews forty years earlier. Now, seeing this troublemaker back on the scene, the Egyptian ruler dismisses Moses's plea as another attempt to stir up trouble among the slaves.

ACCORDING TO GOD'S PLAN

The king's response should have come as no surprise to Moses. "I will harden [pharaoh's] heart so that he will not let the people go," Yahweh had informed his messenger before he left Midian (Exodus 4:21). However, Moses and Aaron may not have explained this fact to the Israelite leaders when they received approval to speak with pharaoh on the Israelites' behalf.

Bricks of Mud and Straw

Bricks made of mud (clay) and straw are perhaps the earliest composite building materials. Ancient builders found that mud bricks were strong when compressed, but broke easily when tension was placed on one edge. Adding straw to the clay before it is dried into bricks provides greater strength when subject to pulling, making a more effective building material. As Philo noted in his *De Vita Mosis* ("Life of Moses"), "straw is the bond which binds bricks together."

In ancient times, bricks were made by packing a wooden frame with a mixture of straw and wet clay. The frame was then lifted, and the process repeated to make another brick. After drying in the sun, the hard bricks could be used to build homes and buildings.

Egyptian tomb paintings from the New Kingdom period depict workers making bricks in this fashion. Brick walls have been found in tombs and other ancient Egyptian structures. However, archaeologists have noted that Egypt also had a supply of stone that was quarried to build its most important monuments, like the pyramids. In Mesopotamia, where stone was not available, brick buildings were more common. As a result, some Biblical critics have speculated that the Exodus stories of Israelite brickmaking in Egypt were inspired by the later enslavement and captivity of the Israelites in Babylon, which occurred after 586 B.C.E.

The Egyptian overseers force the Israelites to gather their own straw, and beat the workers when they are not able to make as many bricks. "Lazy, that's what you are—lazy!" Pharaoh tells the Israelite leaders when they dare to complain about this unfair treatment. "That is why you keep saying, 'Let us go and sacrifice to the Lord.' Now get to work. You will not be given any straw, yet you must produce your full quota of bricks" (Exodus 5:17–18).

The angry Israelites then confront Moses and Aaron, accusing them of making their lives more difficult, rather than delivering them from slavery as promised. Moses is troubled by their accusation, perhaps forgetting that God had already explained how events would unfold. "O Lord, why have you brought trouble upon this people," Moses asks plaintively. "Is this why you sent me? Ever since I went to Pharaoh to speak in your name, he has brought trouble upon this people, and you have not rescued your people at all" (Exodus 5:22–23).

Yahweh instructs Moses to remind the Israelites about the plan He had originally outlined. Unfortunately, the Israelites refuse to listen to Moses. Rather than the strong, decisive leader of popular legend, this chapter of Exodus presents Moses as fainthearted and tentative. Faced with an initial setback, he is ready to drop the entire plan. He tells Yahweh that he'd prefer not to speak with the pharaoh again. "If the Israelites will not listen to me, why would Pharaoh listen to me, since I speak with faltering lips?" he asked (Exodus 6:12).

Showing great patience with this weak man He has chosen as messenger, God responds by outlining in greater detail exactly how events will transpire:

> You are to say everything I command you, and your brother Aaron is to tell Pharaoh to let the

Israelites go out of his country. But I will harden Pharaoh's heart, and though I multiply my miraculous signs and wonders in Egypt, he will not listen to you. Then I will lay my hand on Egypt and with mighty acts of judgment I will bring out my divisions, my people the Israelites. And the Egyptians will know that I am the Lord when I stretch out my hand against Egypt and bring the Israelites out of it (Exodus 7:1–5).

So Moses and Aaron do as God has commanded, and return to the pharaoh's palace. This time, the ruler asks them to perform a miracle as a way to prove there is a divine authority behind their request.

Moses tells Aaron to throw down his staff, and it becomes a snake. Pharaoh is not impressed, however, and he calls in Egyptian magicians to duplicate this feat. The magicians succeeded in turning their own staffs into snakes as well. Even though Aaron's snake then devours the other snakes—demonstrating that his power is greater

Despite the miracle that Moses performs—changing Aaron's staff into a serpent—pharaoh is not impressed.

than that of the other magicians—pharaoh again refuses to listen to Moses's request to allow the Israelites to travel to the wilderness and worship their God.

THE FIRST TWO PLAGUES

Over the next several weeks, therefore, at Moses's direction Yahweh sends a series of calamities, or plagues, to afflict the people of Egypt. The first of these plagues are clearly meant to get people's attention, for they affect the Nile River—the key to the country's economy and its wealth because it is the greatest source of fresh water for agricultural irrigation.

The first plague is one that God had previously described to Moses. He tells Moses, "Tell Aaron, 'Take your staff and stretch out your hand over the waters of Egypt—over the streams and canals, over the ponds and all the reservoirs'—and they will turn to blood. Blood will be everywhere in Egypt, even in the wooden buckets and stone jars" (Exodus 7:19). With a flair for the dramatic, Moses and Aaron walk out to meet pharaoh in the morning, as the ruler walks to the river. Aaron raises his staff, and the water is changed into blood.

Amazingly, pharaoh is unmoved by this sign. He returned to his palace, and ordered the people of Egypt to begin digging wells for fresh water.

The next plague occurs seven days later. Moses says:

> If you refuse to let [my people] go, I will plague your whole country with frogs. The Nile will teem with frogs. They will come up into your palace and your bedroom and onto your bed, into the houses of your officials and on your people, and into your ovens and kneading troughs. The frogs will go up on you and your people and all your officials (Exodus 8:2–4).

When this occurs, the plague is so unpleasant that pharaoh asks for relief. "Pray to the Lord to take the frogs away from me and my people, and I will let your people go to offer sacrifices to the Lord," he tells Moses. Moses responds with confidence: "I leave to you the honor of setting the time for me to pray . . . that you and your houses may be rid of the frogs" (Exodus 8:8, 9). Pharaoh asks for the frogs to be gone the next day, and God, at Moses's request, complies. The invading frogs die and are piled into heaps throughout the land.

Unfortunately for Moses and the Israelites, once the frogs are gone pharaoh changes his mind and refuses to let the Israelites go. This pattern is repeated throughout the encounters between Moses and pharaoh, just as God had promised.

Tormenting the Egyptians

God continues to send plagues to bother the Egyptians. The third plague is a host of gnats, while the fourth is a swarm of biting flies. Miraculously, the gnats and flies do not bother the Israelites, only tormenting the men and animals of Egypt.

Pharaoh, growing tired of these annoyances, summons Moses again and offers him a deal: "Go, sacrifice to your God here in the land." Moses refuses. "That would not be right," he tells the Egyptian ruler. "We must take a three-day journey into the desert to offer sacrifices to the Lord our God, as he commands us" (Exodus 8:25, 26, 27). Pharaoh agrees, and begs Moses to take away the insects. Once again Moses prays and God lifts the plague. And once again, pharaoh reneges on his promise.

Next, God targets the Egyptians' herds of domestic animals. "If you refuse to let [the Israelites] go and continue to hold them back, the hand of the Lord will bring a

The first plague—changing the waters of Egypt to blood—has serious ramifications for a nation that is dependent on irrigated agriculture for its strength. "The fish in the Nile died, and the river smelled so bad that the Egyptians could not drink its water," notes Exodus 7:21.

terrible plague on your livestock in the field—on your horses and donkeys and camels and on your cattle and sheep and goats," Moses tells pharaoh. "But the Lord will make a distinction between the livestock of Israel and that of Egypt, so that no animal belonging to the Israelites will die" (Exodus 9:2–4).

This promise is fulfilled the next day—livestock belonging to the Egyptians that had not been brought into barns dies, but the animals belonging to the Israelites are not affected. Some Egyptian cattle, goats, and other animals do survive this plague, but they will be targeted later.

Because the ancient Egyptians worshipped several animal-headed deities—including the bull-gods Apis and Mnevis, the cow-god Hathor, and the ram-god Khnum—some Biblical commentators have noted that God's destruction of the Egyptians' livestock represents a symbolic attack on Egyptian religious beliefs.

BOILS AND HAILSTONES

Pharaoh refuses to yield, so another plague—festering boils—soon affects the people and the remaining animals of Egypt. Exodus 9:11 says, "The magicians could not stand before Moses because of the boils that were on

"It was the worst storm in all the land of Egypt since it had become a nation," Exodus 9:24–26 says of the seventh plague. "Throughout Egypt hail struck everything in the fields—both men and animals; it beat down everything growing in the fields and stripped every tree. The only place it did not hail was the land of Goshen, where the Israelites were."

them and on all the Egyptians." Some Biblical commentaries believe this means that the boils affected the legs and knees; they therefore link this skin disorder with the punishment for disobeying God that appears in Deuteronomy 28:35—"The Lord will afflict your knees and legs with painful boils that cannot be cured, spreading from the soles of your feet to the top of your head." But even this affliction, which must have brought the commerce and daily life of Egypt to a near-standstill, did not cause pharaoh to change his mind.

The next plague is the worst storm to ever hit Egypt, pounding the earth with hailstones, heavy rain, and thunder and lightning. A day before the storm hits, Moses warns pharaoh to be ready. "Give an order now to bring your livestock and everything you have in the field to a place of shelter," Moses says, "because the hail will fall on every man and animal that has not been brought in and is still out in the field, and they will die" (Exodus 9:19). Some of the Egyptians heed this warning, but most do not; as a result the storm devastates their livestock and their growing crops.

As the storm raged, pharaoh summons Moses again, sounding truly desperate. "This time I have sinned," he says. "The Lord is in the right and I and my people are in the wrong. Pray to the Lord, for we have had enough thunder and hail. I will let you go; you don't have to stay any longer" (Exodus 9:27–28).

Moses agrees to ask God to put an end to the storm, even though by now he knows that pharaoh is only going to change his mind again. "I know that you and your officials still do not fear the Lord God," he told pharaoh (Exodus 9:30). Just as Moses predicts, as soon as the rain and hail stopped, pharaoh goes back on his word again.

A Plague of Locusts

By this point Moses may have been feeling a little frustrated, even though he has been told in advance how events will play out. In the Biblical account God must encourage His messenger to make another visit to pharaoh. Once again, he reminds Moses about His plan: "Go to pharaoh, for I have hardened his heart and the hearts of his officials so that I may perform these miraculous signs of mine among them that you may tell your children and grandchildren how I dealt harshly with the Egyptians and how I performed my signs among them, and that you may know that I am the Lord" (Exodus 10:1-2).

84 *Moses*

The plague of locusts descends upon Egypt. Detail from a 15th-century Bible printed in Germany by Johannes Gutenberg.

Moses returns to the pharaoh and his advisors, warning them that if the Israelites are not permitted to leave Egypt and worship Yahweh in the desert, a vast horde of locusts will descend upon the country and eat whatever trees, crops, and plants were not destroyed by the hailstorm.

Despite God's comment that he will harden the hearts of pharaoh's advisors, they must have remained shaken by the hailstorm as they heard Moses's words. The Bible relates that the advisors urge pharaoh, "Let the people go, so that they may worship the Lord their God. Do you not yet realize that Egypt is ruined?" (Exodus 10:7). Pharaoh seems willing to take this advice, and asks Moses how many of the Israelites are required for the worship service. However, when Moses says that Yahweh requires all of the Israelites to leave Egypt and worship him, pharaoh becomes angry and orders him to get out.

Moses then stretches out his staff, and the wind begins to blow. By the next morning, the locusts have arrived and the sound of insects chewing leaves rumbles throughout Egypt. "Never before had there been such a plague of locusts, nor will there ever be again," notes Exodus 10:14–15. "They covered all the ground until it was black. They devoured all that was left after the hail—everything growing in the fields and the fruit on the trees. Nothing green remained on tree or plant in all the land of Egypt."

Once again, pharaoh asks Moses to end the plague, and once again Moses prays for the plague to stop—and once again, once this is done, pharaoh refuses to allow the Israelites to leave.

Darkness and Death

The ninth plague sent by Yahweh is a darkness that covers all of Egypt. This darkness is unlike any natural eclipse of the sun. First, it lasts for three days; modern scientists say the longest possible duration for a solar eclipse is less than eight minutes. Second, the Bible says that the darkness is so strong that "no one could see anyone else or leave his place for three days" (Exodus 10:23). But even a total solar eclipse is not completely dark—the sun's corona and, often, prominent features like solar flares are visible. Finally, as with the other plagues, the Biblical darkness is selective. Although the Egyptians suffer in darkness for three days, the Israelites in Goshen have light. A midrash recounted in *Legends of the Jews* explains more about the darkness, and how this plague affected the Egyptians:

> The darkness was of such a nature that it could not be dispelled by artificial means. The light of the fire kindled for household uses was either extinguished by the violence of the storm, or else it was made invisible and swallowed up in the density of the darkness. . . . None was able to speak or to hear, nor could anyone venture to take food, but they lay themselves down in quiet and hunger, their outward senses in a trance. Thus they remained, overwhelmed by the affliction, until Moses had compassion on them again, and besought God in their behalf, who granted him the power of restoring fine weather, light instead of darkness and day instead of night.

When the light has been restored, Pharaoh calls for Moses and tells him that all of the Israelites may leave to worship Yahweh. However, the ruler adds, they must leave their livestock behind in Egypt. Moses refuses to accept this condition. "You must allow us to have sacrifices and burnt offerings to present to the Lord our God," he tells pharaoh. "Our livestock too must go with us; not a hoof is to be left behind. We have to use some of them in worshipping the Lord our God, and until we get there we will not know what we are to use to worship the Lord" (Exodus 10:25–26). Pharaoh is livid at this response, and orders Moses out of the palace.

That's okay, Yahweh reassures his mouthpiece, because the time has finally come to unleash the most devastating plague: "About midnight I will go throughout Egypt. Every firstborn son in Egypt will die, from the firstborn son of Pharaoh, who sits on the throne, to the firstborn son of the slave girl, who is at her hand mill, and all the firstborn of the cattle as well. There will be loud wailing throughout Egypt—worse than there has ever been or ever will be again" (Exodus 11:4–6).

But God gives Moses special instructions for the Israelites, which will allow them to protect their children. Each Israelite family is to slaughter a male lamb at twilight, then daub some of the blood onto the posts and lintels at the entrance of their house. "When the Lord goes through the land to strike down the Egyptians, he will see

Natural Explanations?

Many commentators have noted that the first nine plagues could all be explained as natural phenomena. For example, "turning the river to blood" may refer to heavy deposits of reddish silt washed down the Nile from Ethiopia or Central Africa; this silt would have been deadly to river-dwelling fish. Another possible explanation is the occurrence in the Nile of an algal bloom, or "red tide," an event in which the population of microscopic plankton grows rapidly enough to form a visible patch of algae on the water's surface. In large quantities, the plankton present in an algal bloom produces toxins that kill fish, birds, and reptiles.

With the river affected by heavy silt or by a toxic algal bloom, large numbers of frogs would have been forced to leave the poisoned water; these would probably have died. The lack of frogs to help keep the insect population in check may explain the large swarms of flies and gnats. There are biting flies in Egypt that carry diseases like anthrax; these could have been responsible for the livestock deaths, as well as for the boils that afflicted the Egyptians.

Hail and swarms of locusts are both events that occur naturally, and are not uncommon in Egypt even today. Darkness over the land might have been caused by an eclipse or a sandstorm.

Most Jewish and Christian writers acknowledge that the plagues may have had natural causes. The important thing to remember, they note, is that the plagues occurred with unusual rapidity—coming at God's bidding and timing.

The Jewish festival of Passover commemorates the night that the Lord struck down the firstborn sons of Egypt, forcing pharaoh to free the Israelites.

the blood on the top and sides of the doorframe and will pass over that doorway, and he will not permit the destroyer to enter your houses and strike you down," Moses explains to the people (Exodus 12:23).

The Israelites are told to dress as though they are going on a journey, and to eat the lamb roasted, along with bitter herbs and unleavened bread (flat bread that is made without yeast; this type of bread can be made quickly, because it does not require time for the yeast to rise before baking).

The Bible says that the Israelites did as they had been told, and reports what happened:

> At midnight the Lord struck down all the firstborn of Egypt, from the firstborn of Pharaoh, who sat on the throne, to the firstborn of the prisoner, who was in the dungeon, and the firstborn of all the livestock as well. Pharaoh and all his officials and all the Egyptians got up during the night, and there was loud wailing in Egypt, for there was not a house without someone dead (Exodus 12:29–30).

The grieving pharaoh summons Moses again. This time he demands that all of the Israelites leave Egypt with their herds and possessions. Like their ruler, the people of Egypt are happy to see the Israelites preparing to leave. The Egyptians give items of silver and gold, as well as clothing, as gifts to the former slaves.

According to an account by the rabbis recorded in *Legends of the Jews*, Pharaoh and the Egyptians helped the Israelites load their possessions onto wagons, in order to get them out of Egypt as soon as possible:

> When they left, they took with them, beside their own cattle, the sheep and the oxen that Pharaoh had ordered his nobles to give as presents. . . . [The Egyptians] fairly forced raiment upon them, and jewels of silver and jewels of gold, to take along with them on their journey. . . . Indeed, the Israelites bore so much away from Egypt that one of them alone might have defrayed the expense of building and furnishing the Tabernacle.

The Bible doesn't say whether Moses or Aaron received any gifts from the Egyptians. It does note, however, that Moses brought the bones of his ancestor, Joseph, along with him. This was done to fulfill Joseph's dying request, as recorded in Genesis 50:25, "God will surely come to your aid [in Egypt], and then you must carry my bones up from this place."

The Israelites journey to Succoth, a city near the ancient capital of the Hyksos kings of Egypt. From this city—which may have been where they picked up Joseph's bones—the multitude heads into the desert, toward the Red Sea.

MIRACLE AT THE RED SEA

In ancient times, the journey to Canaan, the land Yahweh had promised to the Israelites, would not have been particularly long or difficult. The route was well known. Roads connected Egypt with the city-states of Canaan and continued on to cities in Mesopotamia. Trade caravans and government officials often used these roads. The trip from Egypt to Canaan would have taken an ordinary traveler no more than 12 days.

However, although the Bible says that the Israelites were "armed for battle" when they left Egypt, Moses and Yahweh agreed that the Israelites were not yet ready to fight for Canaan. There is obvious wisdom here: the longer people are beaten down, the harder it becomes for them to fight back against their oppressors. "If they face war, they might change their minds and return to Egypt," Yahweh warns in Exodus 13:17. He instructs Moses to follow a roundabout path when leaving Egypt.

Miracle at the Red Sea 91

As the Israelites prepare to venture into the desert, God appears in an unusual manifestation. During the day, He appears as a pillar of cloud, while at night He shows Himself as a pillar of fire that is bright enough to light their way. This will enable the Israelites to travel either by day or by night, although the Exodus account indicates that most traveling was done by day.

After leaving Succoth, the Israelites encamped briefly at Etham, a city on the edge of the Sinai desert. This settlement is believed to have been located near the modern Egyptian city of Ismaïlia, which is on the Suez Canal.

The people of Israel set out from Egypt, as described in Exodus 12 and 13.

There, Yahweh told Moses:

> Tell the Israelites to turn back and encamp near Pi Hahiroth, between Migdol and the sea. They are to encamp by the sea, directly opposite Baal Zephon. Pharaoh will think, "The Israelites are wandering around the land in confusion, hemmed in by the desert." And I will harden Pharaoh's heart, and he will pursue them. But I will gain glory for myself through Pharaoh and all his army, and the Egyptians will know that I am the Lord" (Exodus 14:2–4).

Pharaoh Prepares for Battle

In Egypt, pharaoh is already regretting the loss of his Israelite slaves. He prepares an army and sets out after the Israelites. The exact size of this army is not mentioned in the Bible. Specific numbers, however, are provided by the Jewish historian Josephus, who had an interest in military matters. Before writing his various historical works, Josephus was a general who led Jewish resistance to the Roman Empire during the first century C.E. "The number that pursued after [the Israelites] was six hundred chariots, with fifty thousand horseman, and two hundred thousand footmen, all armed," Josephus wrote in *Jewish Antiquities*.

The Bible does agree with the figure of 600 chariots, so even if Josephus's other figures are exaggerations, the Egyptian force would have been formidable. The chariot was to ancient warfare what the tank is today: a devastating offensive weapon. The Hyksos rulers had introduced both the chariot and horse to Egypt during the 16th century B.C.E.; these weapons of war had enabled them to gain control of the country. By the New Kingdom period,

Depiction of an Egyptian charioteer from a pharaoh's monument.

the Egyptians had improved the chariot, making it faster, more maneuverable, and more stable.

In ancient times, a chariot was usually drawn by a pair of horses and carried two soldiers. One would attack using spears or a bow and arrow. The other man was the driver, although he could also fight while controlling the horses. The chariot enabled soldiers to move quickly and fire arrows at enemies from a distance. Chariots could then be driven into a melee to trample and crush retreating enemies, while foot soldiers mopped up on the battlefield.

Foot soldiers in the Egyptian army were probably armed with bows and arrows, and may possibly have carried bronze scimitars, battle axes, or daggers. Egyptian soldiers probably carried shields, and may have worn some type of leather armor for protection from enemy attacks. During the New Kingdom, the pharaohs established a professional, full-time army to help them make Egypt a world power. Egyptian soldiers were among the best-trained troops of the ancient world.

In short, the Egyptian army was formidable. As pharaoh's army rumbled toward their camp, it would have stirred up a huge dust cloud that could be seen for miles.

Which Sea Was Crossed?

People who are familiar with the story of Moses know that their Bibles say he parted the waters of the Red Sea in order to let the Israelites cross. However, the sea being referred to is not necessarily the body of water between Africa and the Arabian Peninsula that the modern reader knows as the Red Sea. The original Hebrew text of Exodus refers instead to the Sea of Reeds (Hebrew: *yam sup*), rather than the Red Sea. The error occurred when the Hebrew texts were translated into Greek between the third and first centuries B.C.E.

Modern scholars are uncertain what the Sea of Reeds was, or where it was located. Most speculate that it was a large lake or swamp located somewhere near the Sinai desert. Today, one favored site among Bible historians is Lake Sirbonis, in the Bitter Lakes region to the east of the Nile. This lagoon is fed by the waters of the Mediterranean, and separated from the sea by a narrow strip of land. The area around Lake Sirbonis is marshy; windblown sand gives the impression of dry land where there is boggy territory underneath. If Lake Sirbonis is the *yam sup*, perhaps there is a non-miraculous explanation for the Israelite's miraculous crossing. A person who knew his way could have guided the Israelites through the marsh, while the pursuing Egyptians became stuck in the bog.

Although religious translators have long been aware of the error, most Bibles still use the more familiar "Red Sea" when referring to the incident in which the Israelites crossed the waters to safety.

With a military leader's appreciation for battlefield tactics, Josephus admiringly describes the Egyptian army's maneuvers in his writings. "They . . . seized on the passages by which they imagined the Hebrews might fly, shutting them up between inaccessible precipices and the sea; for there was [on each side] a [ridge of] mountains that terminated at the sea, which were impassable by reason of their roughness, and obstructed their flight."

Not Ready for a Fight

Hemmed in, with the sea to their backs, the Israelites realize there is no escape from this trap. They begin to complain to Moses. "What have you done to us by bringing us out of Egypt," they ask their leader. "It would have been better for us to serve the Egyptians than to die in the desert" (Exodus 14:11, 12). The Israelites' complaints show that God's assessment of His people had been correct: the former slaves are not yet ready to fight even to save themselves. In *Moses: A Life*, Jonathan Kirsch notes:

> Four centuries of slavery had tainted the souls of the Israelites, weakened their will, and left them cowardly, cynical, and calculating. The Israelites were armed, but they dared not fight, even though they vastly outnumbered the Egyptians. After all, six hundred thousand men-at-arms ought to have been able to repulse six hundred chariots. Instead, they complained about the peril into which Moses had led them. At that moment, the clamoring Israelites displayed what would come to be called the slave mentality, a craven spirit that God himself would burn out of the Chosen People with cruel resolve in the days ahead.

Moses attempts to calm the frightened Israelites, reassuring the people that Yahweh will defend them. The

Biblical account presents Moses as resolute and calm. The midrashim note that the leader shows these qualities in public, but they also reveal the private anxiety of Moses. He is depicted as praying strenuously, begging Yahweh to intervene and save the Israelites.

Rather than attempting to establish a defensive line from among the warriors, Moses leads the Israelites toward the sea. In the meantime, the pillar of cloud moves around the Israelite column and blocks the Egyptian army. The Israelite side is bathed in light from the pillar of fire, enabling the people to move forward despite the darkness. However, no light can be seen on the Egyptian side, and the chariots are prevented from pursuing. The midrashim expands on this idea. According to one tale, the frustrated Egyptians fire arrows toward the Israelite camp, but these are blocked by angels in the protective cloud, so that not a single Israelite is harmed.

THE SEA DIVIDED

When Moses reaches the sea, he stretches out his hand. Immediately, a strong east wind begins to blow. The wind is powerful enough to stop the flow of water, creating a dry path through which the Israelites can cross. On either side, the fleeing Israelites can see a wall of water towering over their heads. The ancient historian Philo described the passage through the sea this way:

> [The sea] was broken and divided into two parts, and one of the divisions at the part where it was broken off, was raised to a height and mounted up, and being thus consolidated like a strong wall, stood quiet and unshaken; and the portion behind the Hebrews was also contracted and raised in, and prevented from proceeding forwards, as if it were held back by invisible reins. And the interme-

Miracle at the Red Sea 97

This illustration from a 15th-century German haggadah depicts the crossing of the Red Sea. The image at the top of the page shows pharaoh speaking with his advisors.

The Population Problem

According to the Book of Exodus, about 600,000 Israelite men of fighting age followed Moses out of Egypt. If that figure is correct, then including women, children, and old men the total number of Israelites under Moses's command would have been perhaps 2 million to 2.5 million.

Obviously, this figure presents several problems. First, scholars agree that the entire population of Egypt by the end of the New Kingdom period was less than 4 million; many believe that Egypt's population at that time was probably closer to 3 million. With 600,000 men of fighting age, the Israelites could easily have conquered the land and subjugated the Egyptians, rather than being enslaved by them.

Second, consider the logistics of moving such large numbers of people. For example, if 2 million Israelites walked ten abreast, with less than two feet between the rows, their column would have been more than 110 miles long. If it took just 15 minutes for each row of ten people to cross the river, the Israelite column would have required more than 1,000 hours—42 days—before the last person reached the other side.

Finally, there is no way that the desert could have supported 2 million people, plus their livestock, for a 40-year period. Like other desert nomads, the Israelites would have journeyed from oasis to oasis, pausing at each to water their animals and fill their water skins. There is no archaeological evidence to indicate that the Sinai desert ever hosted a population of millions. Nor is there any evidence that the population of Canaan suddenly increased by 2 million or more people approximately 3,500 years ago.

Some scholars note that the Hebrew word for "thousand," *eleph*, can also be translated to mean "clans" or "military units." If the latter meaning is applied to the Hebrew text, the Israelites would have numbered about 5,000 men of fighting age, and perhaps 20,000 total—figures which seem more realistic to many present-day scholars.

diate space, where the fracture had taken place, was dried up and became a broad, and level, and easy road.

According to the Bible, it takes a single night for the Israelites to cross the sea. At dawn, as the last Israelite reaches the other side, Pharaoh's army arrives on the scene. The Egyptians pursue the fleeing slaves onto the dry path. However, once the army is committed to the crossing, Yahweh tells Moses, "Stretch out your hand over the sea so that the waters may flow back over the Egyptians and their chariots and horsemen" (Exodus 14:26). Moses does as he is told, and the sea immediately rushes back in, engulfing the Egyptian charioteers and soldiers. According to the Bible, not one of them survived.

The account by Josephus gives more details about the scene: "Showers of rain also came down from the sky, and dreadful thunders and lightning, with flashes of fire," he wrote in *Jewish Antiquities*. "Thunderbolts were also darted upon them. . . . And thus did all these men perish, so that there was not one man left to be a messenger of this calamity to the rest of the Egyptians."

Following this miraculous event, the Israelites on the other side of the sea celebrated with singing and dancing. Exodus includes a long psalm, known as the Song of Moses, which celebrates the victory. A shorter fragment, known as the Song of Miriam, is considered by some scholars one of the oldest verses in the Bible. It reads:

> Sing to the Lord
>   for he is highly exalted.
> The horse and its rider
>   He has hurled into the sea (Exodus 15:21).

8

HARDSHIP IN THE DESERT

The Bible and other sources agree that the Israelites celebrate their deliverance from Egypt with singing and dancing. However, according to a folktale recorded by the rabbis, the Israelites also appreciate the opportunity to view the corpses of men who had once abused them. "With their finger they could point them out one by one, saying, 'This was my taskmaster, who beat me with those fists of his at which the dogs are now gnawing, and yonder Egyptian, the dogs are chewing the feet with which he kicked me.'"

According to this tale, the bodies of Egyptian soldiers wash up along the shores of the sea, and the Israelites set to work plundering the bodies. "The sea cast up many jewels, pearls, and other treasures that had belonged to the Egyptians, drowned in its waves," wrote the rabbis, "and Israel found it hard to tear themselves away from the spot that brought them such riches." Moses recognizes that the people will need to carry food and water, not jewelry, as they journey to the promised land. He soon puts a stop to this behavior and starts the people moving again, chiding them: "Do you really believe that the sea will continue to yield you pearls and jewels?"

For several days, the Israelites travel through the desert. They have bread to eat, baked from the unleavened dough that they had brought with them from Egypt, but their water runs out after three days. Finally, the Israelites arrive at an oasis called Marah. However, the water there proves to be bitter and they cannot drink it at first. (The Hebrew word *marah* means "bitter.") Fortunately, God enables Moses to make the water potable by tossing a piece of wood into it. Moving on, the Israelites soon arrive at another oasis, at Elim, where there are a dozen springs and numerous palm trees to provide nourishment for the hungry Israelite host.

FOOD IN THE DESERT

Thus far, Yahweh has provided for his people, but soon after Moses leads the people away from Elim, they begin to complain about his leadership. "If only we had died by the Lord's hand in Egypt!" the people say, according to Exodus 16:3. Proving that the Israelites have exceptionally short memories, they continue: "There we sat around pots of meat and ate all the food we wanted, but you have brought us out into this desert to starve this entire assembly to death."

Moses, the rabbis report, is frustrated by the untruths and complaints about his leadership. He is most annoyed at the peoples' lack of trust in God. "After those many quite extraordinary experiences they had no right to expect merely the natural and the probable, but should cheerfully have trusted [Yahweh]; for, truly, in the sight of all, they had been shown the most tangible proofs of his reliability," notes one midrash.

To stop the complaints, God promises Moses that He will provide food for the entire community. "I have heard the grumbling of the Israelites," God says. "Tell them, 'At twilight you will eat meat, and in the morning you will be filled with bread. Then you will know that I am the Lord your God'" (Exodus 16:12).

That night, a vast multitude of quail lands at the camp. "Toward evening thick swarms of quails came up from the sea, and covered the whole camp, taking their flight quite low . . . so that they might be easily caught," notes one tale.

The next morning, an unusual substance covers the ground around the Israelites' camp. "It is the bread the Lord has given you to eat," explains Moses, as the Israelites examine the strange white flakes. "This is what the Lord has commanded: each one is to gather as much as he needs" (Exodus 16:15–16). Moses tells the Israelites that this bread, which will fall every day except on the Sabbath, is called manna. It will sustain them while they are traveling to the promised land.

The rabbis imagined that manna "had been created on the second day of creation, and ground by the angels. . . . Manna deserves its name, 'bread of the angels,' not only because it is prepared by them, but because those who partake of it become equal to the angels in strength." Another tale says, "throughout forty years . . . manna served them not only as food, but also as provender for their cattle, for the dew that preceded the fall of manna during the night brought grain for their cattle."

Discontent Among the Israelites

The daily provision of manna can be viewed as a sign of God's faithfulness. No matter what His chosen people do,

God tells Moses, "I will rain down bread from heaven for you. The people are to go out each day and gather enough for that day. In this way I will test them and see whether they will follow my instructions. On the sixth day they are to prepare what they bring in, and that is to be twice as much as they gather on the other days" (Exodus 16:4–5). In this painting by the Renaissance artist Lodovico Carracci, Moses watches the Israelites gather manna in the desert.

Yahweh always provides this life-sustaining, miraculous food. Unfortunately, the Israelites do not maintain a faithful attitude toward God, who has rescued them from slavery and continues to work wonders on their behalf. During the long years in the wilderness, the Israelites will constantly complain about the restrictions and commandments that God places upon the people.

Moses, of course, is always the recipient of these complaints, since he is the only person who actually speaks with God. As the community's leader, he must also act as judge when disagreements occur. Thus when the people are discontented, it is Moses against whom they express their anger.

At one point, as the Israelites stop to camp a place in the desert called Rephidim, they complain to Moses that there is no water. Apparently, their grumbling becomes so serious that Moses feels his own life is in danger. The Bible says that Moses cried out to the Lord, "What am I to do with these people? They are almost ready to stone me" (Exodus 17:4).

The Lord responds by telling Moses to perform another miracle. He orders the leader to walk away from the community, with a few of the elders, to a large rock nearby. When Moses strikes the rock with his staff, water flows from it, allowing the people to drink.

This miracle quiets the people for a time, and before the Israelites leave Rephidim Yahweh will present another sign that he is with them.

Defeat of the Amalakites

A tribe living in the region near Rephidim sees the Israelites occupying the oasis and decides to drive them away. These were the Amalekites, a tribe of people who in a way are cousins to the Israelites. Both nations traced their history from the ancient patriarch Abraham, whose son Isaac had two sons of his own. The younger was Jacob, from whom the Israelites were descended. The older son was Esau; he and his descendants became known as the Edomites. Amalek was a grandson of Esau, and settled in the Negev, a desert region in the southern part of modern-day Israel.

Josephus, with his characteristic interest in military matters, calls the Amalekites "the most warlike of the nations that lived around there." He reports that the Amalekites had heard about the Israelites leaving Egypt, and resolved to destroy them before the Israelites could become stronger. "Those who try to crush a power in its first rise, are wiser than those that try to put a stop to its progress when it is become formidable," Josephus comments in *Jewish Antiquities*. "For these last seem to be angry only at the flourishing of others, but the former do not leave any room for their enemies to become troublesome to them."

It is possible that the Israelites had previously skirmished with Amalekites as they were leaving Egypt. This incident is not mentioned in Exodus, but later in his life Moses does allude to a humiliating defeat during a speech: "Remember what the Amalekites did to you along the way when you came out of Egypt," Moses tells the people. "When you were weary and worn out, they met you on your journey and cut off all who were lagging behind; they had no fear of God" (Deuteronomy 25:17–18). Another Biblical reference, from the later Book of Samuel, seems to support this scenario. In this passage, Yahweh tells the prophet Samuel, "I will punish the Amalekites for what they did to Israel when they waylaid them as they came up from Egypt" (1 Samuel 15:2).

Apparently, the Amalekites may have attacked and killed weaker members of the Israelite community, probably women, children, or older people who could not keep up with the larger group. This was a common practice in desert warfare. However, such a massacre would have resulted in a blood feud in which the Israelites would feel bound to destroy the Amalekites. In his Deuteronomy speech, Moses orders his people not to give up the feud until the Amalekites are completely exterminated: "When the Lord your God gives you rest from all the enemies around you in the land he is giving you to possess as an inheritance, you shall blot out the memory of Amalek from under heaven. Do not forget! (Deuteronomy 25:19).

Moses may well have had this earlier defeat in mind when an Amalekite raiding party attacks the Israelite camp at Rephidim. He selects a young Israelite named

Joshua to lead a military response. "Choose some of our men and go out to fight the Amalekites," Moses says. "Tomorrow I will stand on top of the hill with the staff of God in my hands" (Exodus 17:9).

When the battle begins, Moses watches from atop the hill, along with his brother Aaron and an advisor named Hur, a member of the tribe of Judah whom Josephus identifies as the husband of Moses's sister, Miriam. During the fighting a strange phenomenon occurs: as long as Moses holds up his arms toward heaven, the Israelite soldiers are successful in their attack, but whenever he becomes tired and lowers his arms, the Amalekites gain the advantage. To help the Israelites, Aaron and Hur stand on either side of Moses and hold up his arms; at the end of the day, Joshua's forces emerge victorious.

The victory over the Amalekites marks an important transition for the Israelites. As Jonathan Kirsch points out in *Moses: A Life*:

> Something remarkable but often overlooked happened at Rephidim: the Israelites formed themselves into disciplined battalions, closed with a fierce enemy in pitched battle, and held the line without breaking and running. . . . A profoundly new kind of liberation had taken place: the slaves had become warriors, and the warriors had won their first battle. Many more battles would be fought before they claimed the prize that Yahweh had promised them, but none of them would ever forget the day the sword of Israel was first blooded.

The Israelite victory was notable for another reason: it marks the first appearance of Joshua, a brave and remarkable man who would eventually succeed Moses as leader of the Israelites. However, although Joshua led the troops into battle, the rabbis give Moses credit for the triumph. "Only through the aid of Moses did Joshua win his victory. Moses did not go out into battle, but through prayer and through his influence upon the people in inspiring them with faith, the battle was won," wrote the rabbis.

According to Josephus, the victory also makes the Israelites wealthy, adding to the plunder they had taken from the Egyptians:

> When they had taken the enemy's camp, they got ready booty . . . whereas until then they had not any sort of plenty, of even necessary food. . . . For they . . . made slaves of the bodies of their enemies. . . . Moreover, they acquired a vast quantity of riches; for a great deal of silver and gold was left in the enemy's camp. . . . They also got the spoils of their cattle.

MOSES IS REUNITED WITH HIS FAMILY

Soon after this battle, Moses is reunited with his wife and family. The Bible reports that stories about the Israelites' successes spread throughout the region. The news eventually reaches Midian, where Moses's wife Zipporah and their two sons have been living with her father, Jethro, since Moses went to Egypt. It is at this point in the Exodus account that readers learn the name of Moses's second son, Eliezer. The boy's name means "God helps," for Moses had commented, "God was my helper; he saved me from the sword of pharaoh" (Exodus 18:4).

Jethro, Zipporah, and the two boys travel through the desert to meet the Israelites, and Moses is delighted to see them. When Moses describes the Israelites' adventures, Jethro is so impressed that he tells his son-in-law, "Now I know that the Lord is greater than all other gods" (Exodus

18:11). Jethro then apparently accepts Yahweh as his God, for he prepares a ritual sacrifice with Moses, Aaron, and the Israelite leaders.

The Midianites were pagans, and Jethro had previously been described as "a priest of Midian" (Exodus 2:16), so his willingness to pay homage to Yahweh marks a surprising change. In fact, he appears more impressed by Yahweh's miracles and expressions of power than the complaining Israelites do. At the same time, Jethro does not admit that Yahweh is the only god, just that he is the greatest of all gods. Moses does not press the issue.

According to some Bible scholars, this incident of a sacrifice, followed by a meal with Jethro and the Israelite leaders, may have sealed a sort of alliance between the Midianites and the Israelites. Unlike the Amalekites, the Midianites do not attack the Israelites. They allow the Israelites to travel through their territory in peace. Unfortunately, the peace between the Israelites and the Midianites will not last; near the end of Moses's life, he sends an army to destroy Midianite cities in the valley of Moab. Later, during the time the Israelites were fighting to subdue Canaan, a judge named Gideon leads the Israelites to a decisive victory over these allies-turned-enemies. "Thus Midian was subdued before the Israelites and did not raise its head again," notes Judges 8:28.

The archaeological evidence of a civilization that flourished in Midian during the 13th and 12th centuries, coupled with the Biblical report of Gideon's war against the people and the apparent destruction of Midianite civilization, lends credence to the theory that stories and traditions about Moses existed in oral form long before state of Israel was established in the 10th century B.C.E. As Lawrence E. Stager writes in *The Oxford History of the Biblical World*, "It strains credulity to think that traditions about Moses, the great lawgiver and hero who married the daughter of the priest of Midian, were created during or after these hostilities."

Ruling the Israelites

Jethro also provides Moses another important service: he instructs him in the ways of governing a nomadic tribe. The day after the sacrifice ritual, Jethro sees Moses deeply involved in resolving disputes among the people. Jethro tells Moses that he has to create a better administrative system in order to rule the Israelites properly. "What you are doing is not good," Jethro says:

> You and these people who come to you will only wear yourselves out. The work is too heavy for you; you cannot handle it alone. Listen now to me and I will give you some advice, and may God be with you. You must be the people's representative before God and bring their disputes to Him. Teach them the decrees and laws, and show them the way to live and the duties they are to perform. But select capable men from all the people—men who fear God, trustworthy men who hate dishonest gain—and appoint them as officials over thousands, hundreds, fifties, and tens. Have them serve as judges for the people at all times, but have them bring every difficult case to you; the simple cases they can decide themselves. That will make your load lighter, because they will share it with you. If you do this and God so commands, you will be able to stand the strain, and all these people will go home satisfied (Exodus 18:17–23).

The Bible says that Moses listened to his father-in-law and did everything he suggested, choosing capable men and establishing them as judges. And Yahweh would soon provide detailed laws and decrees that would create the framework enabling Moses and his administrators to rule.

THE COMMANDMENTS OF THE LORD

Three months after the Israelites left Egypt, they arrive at Mount Sinai, a high place where Yahweh is said to dwell. It is on Mount Sinai that Yahweh will give Moses laws for the Israelite community; these laws become part of God's covenant with His chosen people. "Now if you obey me fully and keep my covenant, then out of all nations you will be my treasured possession," Yahweh promises. "Although the whole earth is mine, you will be for me a kingdom of priests and a holy nation" (Exodus 19:5–6).

The actual location of Mount Sinai is uncertain. Christian tradition places it in the high mountains of the southern Sinai Peninsula, a peak that today is known as Jebel Musa (Mountain of Moses). However, some modern scholars and archaeologists believe that Mount Sinai may not have been located in the Sinai Peninsula at all, but on the Arabian Peninsula.

Wherever Mount Sinai is located, God makes clear that it is a holy place. "Put limits for the people around the mountain and tell them, 'Be careful that you do not go up the mountain and touch the foot of it,'" Yahweh tells Moses. "Whoever touches the mountain shall surely be put to death" (Exodus 19:12).

Following God's instructions, Moses prepares the people. Three days after arriving in the vicinity of Mount Sinai, the Israelites are treated to the spectacle of Yahweh's presence descending on the mountain. The top of Mount Sinai is wreathed in smoke and flame, accompanied by the sound of thunder, lightning, and the sound of trumpets. Then Yahweh orders Moses to the top of the mountain, where He will hand down the laws.

Since the fourth century C.E., Christians have identified Jebel Musa, in the southern Sinai Peninsula, as the place where Moses received the Ten Commandments. Around 330 C.E. the Roman emperor Constantine's mother, Helena, made a celebrated pilgrimage to the Holy Land to identify places where important events described in the Bible had taken place. At her direction a small church was built on the northwest slope of Jebel Musa to mark the spot where Moses received the laws from Yahweh.

The first and most important of these laws, of course, are the Ten Commandments, which have become embodied in the moral and legal codes of modern western civilization. Many Biblical scholars believe that the Ten Commandments are among the oldest, most authentic texts in the Bible. This is because of their format: the commandments provide specific and absolute prohibitions ("you shall have no other gods before me," "You shall not murder"). By contrast, many of the 613 laws included in the Torah are conditional, following an "if-then" format. For example, Exodus 21:20–21: "If a man beats his male or female slave with a rod and the slave dies as a direct result, he must be punished, but he is not to be punished if the slave gets up after a day or two, since the slave is his property." This "if-then" pattern is found in other legal codes from the ancient Middle East, such as the Code of Hammurabi (circa 1760 B.C.E.).

Moses is instructed to write down the commandments, as well as other laws related to personal injuries, the treatment of servants, the protection of property, social responsibilities, and religious practice. He then returns to the Israelites and sets up an altar at the foot of Mount Sinai. Moses reveals Yahweh's commandments to the people, and they respond, "We will do everything the Lord has said; we will obey" (Exodus 24:7). Moses then performs a ritual to seal the agreement.

RECEIPT OF THE STONE TABLETS

After this, God calls Moses back up to the top of Mount Sinai. Moses places Aaron and Hur in charge of the people, and spends the next forty days on the mountaintop in close conversation with Yahweh. According to the Biblical account, Moses receives many other decrees from Yahweh during this time, including detailed instructions on religious rituals, such as the appropriate construction of altars, the proper clothing for priests, and the correct way to offer animal sacrifices to the Lord. Yahweh also provides directions for the construction of a sanctuary and for the Ark of the Covenant, where documents related to the covenant can be stored.

The rabbis imagined that God spent the time tutoring Moses in all of the intricacies and complexities of His law. "The forty days that Moses spent in heaven were entirely devoted to the study of the Torah," writes Louis Ginzberg. "He learned the written as well as the oral teaching, yea, even the doctrines that an able scholar would someday propound were revealed to him."

Hardship in the Desert 113

Unfortunately, while Moses was away the Israelites grew restless. The people soon prove ready to abandon Yahweh and worship other gods. The tell Aaron, "make us gods who will go before us" (Exodus 32:1).

Hur's role in this incident is not mentioned in the Bible, but according to the midrashim, he is killed because he refuses to acquiesce to the people's demands. This may explain Aaron's subsequent willingness to be involved in the plot. Aaron tells the Israelites to bring him all of their gold jewelry. Some commentators have attempted to excuse Aaron by saying that he hoped this demand would be too much for the people, because they wouldn't want to give up their riches. But the people agree to Aaron's demand and turn over their jewelry. At Aaron's direction the gold is then melted down and formed into the shape of a calf, or a young bull.

According to Jewish folktales, this time on the mountain not only enriched Moses spiritually, it also provided him with material wealth. One story holds that as God inscribed the Ten Commandments and the other laws onto two stone tablets, the chips that fell from the stone turned to diamonds and rubies.

This gold-plated bronze young bull, representing the Canaanite god Baal, was found in modern-day Lebanon. Many cultures of the ancient Middle East, including the Egyptians and the tribes of Canaan, held bulls in high regard. The animals were sometimes worshipped as symbols of fertility and power, and were also commonly used as sacrifices to other deities. Without Moses to keep order in their camp, the Israelites may have been reverting to a form of worship they had practiced in Egypt.

Aaron then erects an altar in front of the calf, and the next day a festival is held. The Bible reports that "the people rose early and sacrificed burnt offerings. . . . Afterward they sat down to eat and drink and got up to indulge in revelry" (Exodus 32:6).

When Yahweh looks down from Mount Sinai, and sees the orgy that is taking place and the way his chosen people have turned from him so quickly, he becomes extremely angry. He decides to destroy the faithless Israelites, and he offers to make a new covenant with Moses and his descendants:

"I have seen these people," the Lord said to Moses, "and they are a stiff-necked people. Now leave me alone so that my anger may burn against them and that I may destroy them. Then I will make you into a great nation" (Exodus 32:9–10).

But Moses argues for the people, attempting to save them from the destruction that they deserve. To sway Yahweh, he appeals to His pride. "Why should the Egyptians say, 'It was with evil intent that he brought them out, to kill them in the mountains and to wipe them off the face of the earth," Moses pleads. "Turn from your fierce anger; relent and do not bring disaster on your people" (Exodus 32:12).

Yahweh agrees not to destroy the Israelites; instead, he sends Moses back down the mountain to their camp with the two stone tablets containing the laws. On the way down, Moses meets his aide Joshua, who apparently has been waiting for him and does not know what has occurred. As they proceed down the mountain, Joshua hears loud, strange noises and become concerned that the Israelites are fighting a battle. But as they draw closer, Moses sees that the Israelites are dancing before the golden calf.

The man who had begged God to hold back his wrath cannot stop his own angry response. Moses throws the tablets down and they shatter on the mountainside. Then he sweeps into camp, knocks over the golden calf and destroys the idol. Next, he chastises Aaron for leading the people into sin. Moses calls on those who are faithful to Yahweh to kill the Israelites who are engaged in idol worship. The Levites respond with their swords, and the Bible reports that they kill about 3,000 of the apostates.

"The episode of the Golden Calf proves that, for most people, faith and doubt exist independently of anything that God does," writes Rabbi Joseph Telushkin. "Although every promise Moses had made in God's name was fulfilled, that was not enough to keep the Israelites faithful for more than forty days. What makes us so sure we would be any different?"

The Tent of Meeting

His anger abated, Yahweh tells Moses to lead the people toward Canaan. First, though, He orders Moses back to the top of Mount Sinai, where He provides two new stone tablets with the law carved into them. These are to replace the tablets that Moses had smashed when he found the Israelites worshipping the golden calf.

This sculpture of Moses by Michelangelo depicts the great lawgiver with two horns emerging from his head. This is a common feature in depictions of Moses, and stems from a poor translation of Exodus 34. The Hebrew word qaran is used to describe the appearance of Moses after he came down from Mount Sinai with the tablets. This word is derived from the Hebrew word for "horn," but was also used as an expression meaning "to radiate with light." When the fourth century Christian priest/scholar Jerome translated Exodus and other books of the Torah into Latin, he misunderstood the idiom. Thus, the Vulgate translation—the version of the Bible used by nearly all Christians until the Protestant Reformation of the 16th century—says, "the skin of [Moses's] face <u>sent forth horns</u>." As a result, it became common for artists during and after the Renaissance to show Moses with horns.

When Moses returns to the Israelites' camp, he is surprised to find the people shocked and fearful. "[Moses] was not aware that his face was radiant because he had spoken with the Lord," reports the Bible. "When Aaron and all the Israelites saw Moses, his face was radiant, and they were afraid to come near him. But Moses called to them; so Aaron and all the leaders of the community came back to him, and he spoke to them" (Exodus 34:29–31).

Moses speaks with the people once again about God's laws and commandments. He also explains that the Lord will accompany the Israelites as they set out from Mount Sinai for the promised land, Canaan. Moses directs Israelites who are skilled at working with wood, precious metals, gemstones, wool and fabric, and other materials to construct an elaborate Tent of Meeting, or tabernacle, where he will speak with the Lord during the Israelites' journey. The tabernacle includes the Ark of the Covenant, a gold-covered box where the tablets containing the law were stored. When all is complete, Exodus 40:34–38 reports:

> Then the cloud covered the Tent of Meeting, and the glory of the Lord filled the tabernacle. Moses could not enter the Tent of Meeting because the cloud had settled upon it, and the glory of the Lord filled the tabernacle.
> In all the travels of the Israelites, whenever the cloud lifted from above the tabernacle, they would set out; but if the cloud did not lift, they did not set out—until the day it lifted. So the cloud of the Lord was over the tabernacle by day, and fire was in the cloud by night, in the sight of all the house of Israel during all their travels.

9

LEADER OF HIS PEOPLE

A longstanding tradition holds that Moses was the author of the Torah, or Pentateuch, which corresponds to the first five books of the Christian Old Testament. Orthodox Jews and many Christians believe Moses actually wrote these books himself during the time that the Israelites wandered in the desert. They point to passages like the following, from Exodus and Deuteronomy, as proof that Moses put pen to papyrus:

> Moses then wrote down everything the Lord had said.... Then he took the Book of the Covenant and read it to the people. They responded, "We will do everything the Lord has said; we will obey" (Exodus 24:4, 7).
>
> Then the Lord said to Moses, "Write down these words, for in accordance with these words I have made a covenant with you and with Israel."... And he wrote on the tablets the words of

the covenant—the Ten Commandments (Exodus 34:27, 28).

So Moses wrote down this law and gave it to the priests, the sons of Levi, who carried the ark of the covenant of the Lord, and to all the elders of Israel (Deuteronomy 31:9).

To support their belief in Moses as the author of the scriptures, Christians also cite a passage from the New Testament Gospel of John, in which Jesus Christ tells Jewish leaders, "If you believed Moses, you would believe me, for he wrote about me. But since you do not believe what he wrote, how are you going to believe what I say?" (John 5:46–47).

THE DOCUMENTARY HYPOTHESIS

On the other hand, nearly all secular scholars of the Bible believe that numerous people contributed to the first five books of the Bible, and that the books were written, edited, and revised over hundreds of years. Richard Elliott Friedman, an influential Bible historian and critic, says, "There is hardly a biblical scholar in the world actively working on the problem who would claim that the Five Books of Moses were written by Moses—or by any one person."

During the late 19th century, a theory of Biblical authorship called the Documentary Hypothesis was formulated. Over the years there have been numerous variations on this theory. In its simplest form, the Documentary Hypothesis says that the main blocks of stories in the books of Genesis and Exodus—including the story of Noah—are the oldest material. They are attributed to two anonymous authors, known as J and E. The initials come from the names for God that each author uses in the narrative—J for "Yahweh" (in German, the language of Julius Wellhausen, the scholar who originally formulated the hypothesis, "Jahweh") and E for "Elohim." Scholars believe these two sets of stories were written down between 950 and 800 B.C.E., although they probably existed in oral form much earlier than that.

Around 600 B.C.E., new material concerned with religious or legal matters—such as the covenant between God and Abraham in Genesis 17, along with genealogical information—was added. This material is believed to have been the work of a priest or group of priests, and is labeled P.

The first five books of the Bible were placed in their final form around 400 B.C.E. by a group of editors, who blended the J, E, and P strands together and added new material. The addition is labeled R, after the group of

Scholars believe that stories about Moses in the Torah may first have been written down during the time of King Solomon, around 950 B.C.E., and that these stories were probably edited and expanded until about 400 B.C.E.—about a thousand years after Moses is believed to have lived.

redactors who are believed to have concentrated on reworking and polishing the text.

Over the past two centuries the Biblical text has been the subject of intense scholarly scrutiny. This theory offers an understanding of how the Book of Genesis might have been composed. However, there are still numerous points of disagreement among scholars, and many of them may be impossible to ever resolve.

That is not to reduce Moses's importance, however. Moses is by far the most important figure, with a large portion of the text related to his life and works. Many scholars believe a "Mosaic core" that reflects his ancient teachings is preserved in the contemporary Biblical text. As David J. A. Clines, a professor of Biblical studies at the University of Sheffield, England, explains, "Whether or not Moses can be called the author in a literal sense of anything in the Pentateuch, it is reasonable to hold that his work and teaching were the initial stimulus for the creation of the Pentateuch."

WANDERING IN THE WILDERNESS

The Book of Exodus provides a straightforward narrative account of Moses's life and the rescue of the Israelites, ending with the nation departing from Mount Sinai. The rest of Moses's story is told in the three books of the Pentateuch that follow: Leviticus, Numbers, and Deuteronomy. These three books are very different from Exodus, however.

Leviticus, which means "about the Levites," primarily describes the proper procedures for sacrifices, worship, annual festivals, and ritual cleanliness that God's priests are required to follow. Although the laws are meant to provide guidance to the priests, the entire Israelite community is expected to observe the restrictions. "I am the

Lord your God; concecrate yourselves and be holy, because I am holy," Yahweh commands in Leviticus 11:44.

The book also mentions events that occur in the Israelite community that reflect how important it is to obey God's law. For example, Leviticus 8 and 9 describes Aaron and his sons being ordained as priests. In the next chapter, Aaron's sons Nadab and Abihu attempt to offer an unacceptable sacrifice. "So fire came out from the presence of the Lord and consumed them, and they died before the Lord," notes Leviticus 10:2. Another story, in Leviticus 24:10–25, describes how the Israelites stone a person who curses God.

The Book of Numbers gets its name from the censuses, or numberings of the people of Israel, which occur in chapters 1 and 26. The first part of the book (chapters 2 through 10) provide more details about the Israelite camp at Mount Sinai. The remainder of the book discusses the journey from Mount Sinai to the east side of the Dead Sea—a trip that takes some 38 years and involves many problems for Moses. In one case, fire from the Lord consumes some Israelites who are complaining (again) about their troubles. Moses also has to put down several revolts among the discontented people—one of them led by his siblings Aaron and Miriam.

At God's command, Moses sends spies to explore Canaan. The spies return with fruit from the land, and tell the Israelites, "We went into the land to which you sent us, and it does flow with milk and honey! . . . But the people who live there are powerful, and the cities are fortified and very large. . . . We can't attack thoes people; they are stronger than we are" (Numbers 13:27, 28, 31). Only two of the spies—Moses's aide Joshua and a man named Caleb—are prepared to do as God has commanded: march into Canaan and take possession of the land.

Another rebellion breaks out in the Israelite camp, and this time the Lord becomes extremely angry. "How long will these people treat me with contempt?" He rages to Moses in the Tent of Meeting. "How long will they refuse to believe in me, in spite of all the miraculous signs I have performed among them? I will strike them down with a plague and destroy them, but I will make you into a nation greater and stronger than they" (Numbers 14:11–12).

Moses pleads for God to forgive the people, and God agrees not to wipe out the Israelites. However, he does have a punishment in mind:

> Nevertheless, as surely as I live and as surely as the glory of the Lord fills the whole earth, not one of the men who saw my glory and the miraculous signs I performed in Egypt and in the desert but who disobeyed me and tested me ten times—not one of them will ever see the land I promised on oath to their forefathers. No one who has treated me with contempt will ever see it. But because my servant Caleb has a different spirit and follows me wholeheartedly, I will bring him into the land he went to, and his descendants will inherit it. Since the Amalekites and Canaanites are living in the valleys, turn back tomorrow and set out toward the desert along the route to the Red Sea. (Numbers 14:21–25)

According to one midrash, God's punishment of the Israelites comes with a silver lining for their children. "At the time when Israel departed from Egypt, Palestine was in poor condition; the trees planted in the time of Noah were old and withered. Hence God said: "What! Shall I permit Israel to enter an uninhabitable land? I shall bid them wander in the desert for forty years, that the Canaanites may in the meantime fell the old trees and plant new ones, so that Israel, upon entering the land, may find it abounding in plenty." This tale goes on to say that the Canaanites were misers who hoarded their olive oil and other resources; when the Israelites do conquer the land, they gain these possessions to enjoy and use.

Continued Rebellion

The next day, the Lord kills the spies who had warned against attacking the Canaanites. The Israelites mourn, and acknowledge that they have sinned against the Lord. Some of them even want to enter Canaan—even though now God has told them not to. Moses warns the people that they will be defeated, because they are not obeying God's will. "Because you have turned away from the Lord, He will not be with you and you will fall by the sword," he says in Numbers 14:43. Nonetheless, this group of rebellious Israelites persists, and is wiped out by the Amalekites and Canaanites in the hill country.

The fate of rebels against God's commands and Moses's leadership seems clear. Yet the grumbling in the Israelite camp does not stop. A Levite named Korah plots with more than 200 elders of the community to overthrow Moses and Aaron. When Korah and his associates openly challenge Moses's leadership, Yahweh causes the earth to open and swallow the plotters. Another group of conspirators, led by Dathan and Abiram, are consumed by fire.

During the years of wandering, the older Israelites gradually begin to die off. Moses's sister Miriam dies when the community arrives at a place in the desert called Kadesh. It is here that even Moses falters in his obedience to the Lord. According to the Bible, there is no water at Kadesh for the Israelite community, so the Israelite community begins to grumble again. The Lord tells Moses and Aaron to assemble the people around a large rock, then command the rock to pour forth water. Moses does as he has told, but instead of speaking to the rock he hits it twice with his staff. The Lord does allow the water to flow forth, satisfying the peoples' needs. However, he is not pleased that Moses did not follow his exact directions. "Because you did not trust in Me enough to honor me as holy in the sight of the Israelites, you will not bring this community into the land I give them," God tells Moses (Numbers 20:12). Soon after this, Aaron dies and his son Eleazar is invested as Israel's high priest.

GOING TO WAR

As the period of wandering draws toward its end, the Israelites begin to come into conflict with the nations that

Numbers 21 describes how Yahweh becomes angry about the Israelites' continued grumbling and sends venomous snakes among them. When the people repent, God tells Moses to make a bronze serpent and put it on a pole. Anyone who is bitten and looks at the serpent will live. Creation of the bronze serpent—called in Jewish tradition the Nehushtan—seems to be a violation of the commandment prohibiting idols. However, the Bible indicates that the Nehushtan was kept after Moses's death, along with other relics. It was eventually destroyed by the reforming king Hezekiah during the eighth century B.C.E. because the Israelites are worshipping the serpent; Hezekiah's actions are described in 2 Kings 18:4.

live around Canaan. From Kadesh, Moses asks the king of Edom to allow his people to pass through Edomite territory. He promises peace, but the Edomite ruler refuses and the Israelites must journey around Edom. The Israelites are attacked by the Canaanite king of Arad, and in response destroy their cities. They also defeat the armies of the Amorite kings Sihon and Og, and take possession of their territories.

Ultimately, the Israelites camp in the plains of Moab, on the eastern side of the Jordan River. The Moabite king Balak tries to drive them away, hiring a sorcerer named Balaam for this purpose. But God orders Balaam not to act against the Israelites, and he returns home.

The Moabite and Midianite women have more success than the men, however. They seduce the Israelite men, and encourage them to worship idols. Some of the Israelites worship a local deity called the Baal of Peor.

Yahweh orders Moses to kill the people involved in idol worship. Moses directs the leaders of each tribe to carry out this order. The Bible says that 24,000 Israelites are killed before the Lord's anger abates.

God then says to Moses, "Treat the Midianites as enemies and kill them, because they treated you as enemies

---

Chapter 33 of the Book of Numbers gives a detailed chronology of the Israelite journey through the wilderness. The text says that Moses recorded the various stages of the journey; contemporary scholars who agree with the documentary hypothesis typically ascribe authorship of the text to the Priestly source, who is believed to have written in the sixth century B.C.E.

when they deceived you in the affair of Peor" (Numbers 25:17). Moses takes a census of the people, finding more than 601,000 Israelite men in the community. He commissions an army of 12,000 men—a thousand from each tribe—and sets out to fight the Midianites. The Israelites win an easy victory over the five kings of Midian. They kill the Midianite men, burn the towns and villages of the region, and capture the women and children, along with their livestock and possessions.

Moses then orders the Israelites to kill the male children and the married women. Young virgin girls are permitted to live; they will be incorporated into the Israelite community. In *Moses: A Life*, Jonathan Kirsch comments on this harsh order:

> The slaughter of Midianite women and children is rationalized in pious tradition as a justified punishment for the scheme "to seduce the sons of Israel to unchastity and then to idolatry." . . . And yet the Bible seems to acknowledge that the mass murder of the captive women and their young sons was something far beyond the justifiable bloodshed of a holy war, something that scarred and tainted the men who were commanded by Moses to carry out the killings.

After the massacre, Moses insists that his soldiers must undergo a complicated ritual to cleanse themselves. "All of you who have killed anyone or touched anyone who was killed must stay outside the camp seven days," he says. "On the third and seventh days you must purify yourselves and your captives. Purify every garment as well as everything made of leather, goat hair, or wood" (Numbers 31:19–20).

THE DEATH OF MOSES

With the destruction of Midian, the Israelites appear to be ready to enter Canaan. By this time, Moses, Caleb, and Joshua are the only surviving members of the Israelite community that left Egypt 40 years earlier. Yahweh tells Moses, "Go up this mountain in the Abarim range and see the land I have given the Israelites. After you have seen it, you too will be gathered to your people" (Numbers 27:12–13).

Moses is told to place his aide, Joshua, in charge of the community. He does this in a public ceremony, accompanied by Eleazar the high priest.

The word *Deuteronomy* means "second law." Much of the book is made up of two speeches made by Moses to the Israelites around this time. Before the people entered Canaan, Moses wants to remind them of all that God had done for them. He also wants to go over the Ten Commandments and other laws that the people will have to obey in order to remain in God's favor.

When Moses is finished, he climbs Mount Nebo. From this high place, he can see the entire land of Canaan. The Bible reports Moses's death:

> And Moses the servant of the Lord died there in Moab, as the Lord had said. He buried him in Moab, in the valley opposite Beth Peor, but to this day no one knows where his grave is. Moses was a hundred and twenty years old when he died, yet his eyes were not weak nor his strength gone. The Israelites grieved for Moses in the plains of Moab thirty days, until the time of weeping and mourning was over. . . .
>
> Since then, no prophet has risen in Israel like Moses, whom the Lord knew face to face, who did all those miraculous signs and wonders the Lord

sent him to do in Egypt—to Pharaoh and to all his officials and to his whole land. For no one has ever shown the mighty power or performed the awesome deeds that Moses did in the sight of all Israel (Deuteronomy 34:5–8, 10–12).

MOSES TODAY

Unlike the literature of some other ancient Middle Eastern cultures, the Bible does not present Moses as a one-dimensional character—a brave and confident hero who rescues his people from slavery. Instead, the Moses of the Bible and the related folklore has very human characteristics. He is at different times proud and humble, brave and fearful, confident and indecisive. The Moses of the Bible has great ability, but he is not without flaws—just like any great leader of human history. Some people believe this realistic portrayal reflects the fact that Moses did in fact exist.

Others, however, believe that Moses's rich and complex character simply reflects the manner in which the Bible was composed. Most secular Bible scholars—those who consider the Bible a work of human authors and study it from a literary or historical perspective—believe that many of the stories included in the Torah were passed down orally for centuries before being written down, and that many different people were involved in writing and editing the texts between about 950 and 400 B.C.E.

One day, archaeological or documentary evidence may prove definitively whether Moses really lived. Until then, those who are interested will have to look at the available evidence and decide for themselves. In the meantime, the life of Moses continues to provide a guide to how every person can live in the way that God prefers.

Notes

CHAPTER 1: MOSES THE MILLIONAIRE

p. 13: "Moses is regarded not only. . ." Louis Ginzberg, *Legends of the Jews*, vol. 1 (Philadelphia: The Jewish Publication Society, 2003), p. 545.

p. 16: "Moses spent his first forty . . ." Dwight L. Moody, quoted in Henrietta C. Mears, *What the Bible Is All About* (Ventura, Calif.: Gospel Light Publications, 1966), p. 33.

p. 17: "If you're making up history . . ." Quoted in Jeffery Sheler, *Is the Bible True? How Modern Debates and Discoveries Affirm the Essence of the Scriptures* (New York: HarperCollins/Zondervan, 1999), p. 78.

CHAPTER 2: THE ISRAELITES IN EGYPT

p. 19: "The Apiru plunder . . . " J. Maxwell Miller and John H. Hayes, *A History of Ancient Israel and Judah* (Philadelphia: Westminster Press, 1986), p. 66.

p. 21: "the gift of the Nile," Herodotus, *The Histories*, John M. Marincola, ed., trans. Aubery de Selincourt (New York: Penguin Classics, 2003), p. 140.

p. 22: "I was in distress . . ." James A. Pritchard, ed. *Ancient Near Eastern Texts Relating to the Old Testament* (Princeton, N.J.: Princeton University Press, 1955), p. 31.

p. 27: "The dislike of the Egyptians . . . " C.F. Keil and F. Delitzsch, *Biblical Commentary on the Old Testament*, trans. James Martin (Grand Rapids, Mich.: William B. Eerdmans Publishing Company, n.d.), p. 375.

p. 28:   "Bedouin have kept..." Charles F. Pfeiffer, *Old Testament History* (Washington, D.C.: Canon Press, 1973), p. 131.

p. 31:   "Canaan is captive..." William G. Dever, *Who Were the Early Israelites and Where Did they Come From?* (Grand Rapids, Mich.: William B. Eerdmans, 2002), p. 202.

p. 34:   "day and night without interruption..." Philo of Alexandria, *The Works of Philo*, trans. C. D. Yonge. (Peabody, Mass.: Hendrickson Publishers, 1993), p. 462–463.

p. 37:   "When they discovered one..." Ginzberg, *Legends of the Jews*, vol. 1, p. 472.

CHAPTER 3: THE BIRTH AND EARLY LIFE OF MOSES

p. 42:   "I have brought up a child..." Ginzberg, *Legends of the Jews*, vol. 1, p. 481.

p. 43:   "If it please the king..." Ginzberg, *Legends of the Jews*, vol. 1, p. 483.

p. 44:   "For all of his life..." Ginzberg, *Legends of the Jews*, vol. 1, p. 483.

p. 46:   "The Egyptian school system..." Pfeiffer, *Old Testament History*, p. 151.

p. 47:   "And he tamed, and appeased..." Philo of Alexandria, *The Works of Philo*, p. 461.

p. 48:   "He came upon the Ethiopians..." Flavius Josephus, *The New Complete Works of Josephus*, trans. by William Whitson (Grand Rapids, Mich.: Kregel Publications, 1999), p. 100.

p. 48:   "happened to see Moses..." Josephus, *The New Complete Works of Josephus*, p. 100.

CHAPTER 4: INTO THE WILDERNESS

p. 49:   "After he had left..." Gregory of Nyssa, *The Life of Moses* (New York: HarperCollins, 2006), p. 9.

p. 50:   "He dismissed all thought..." Ginzberg, *Legends of the Jews*, vol. 1, p. 485.

p. 50:   "It is an admitted fact..." Ginzberg, *Legends of the Jews*, vol. 1, p. 486.

p. 52: "take occasion from his..." Josephus, *The New Complete Works of Josephus*, p. 101.

p. 53: "[B]ecause the public roads..." Josephus, *The New Complete Works of Josephus*, p. 101.

p. 55: "a man with insight..." Gregory of Nyssa, *The Life of Moses*, p. 10.

p. 55: "saw in one act..." Gregory of Nyssa, *The Life of Moses*, p. 10.

p. 55: "[Reuel] appointed him..." Josephus, *The New Complete Works of Josephus*, p. 101.

p. 56: "Moses took his father-in-law's..." Philo of Alexandria, *The Works of Philo*, p. 464.

p. 56: "By the way [Moses] tended..." Ginzberg, *Legends of the Jews*, vol. 1, p. 500.

p. 58: "During the forty years..." Ginzberg, *Legends of the Jews*, vol. 1, p. 500.

CHAPTER 5: MESSAGE FROM A BURNING BUSH

p. 66: "While Moses was receiving..." J. Frederic McCurdy and Kaufmann Kohler, "Aaron," JewishEncyclopedia.com. http://www.jewishencyclopedia.com/view.jsp?artid=4&letter=A&search=aaron#0

p. 68: "What did all this mean..." Charles R. Swindoll, *Moses: A Man of Selfless Dedication* (Nashville, Tenn.: Word Publishing, 1999), p. 125.

p. 69: "The fact that..." Charles Pfeiffer, *Old Testament History*, p. 98.

p. 70: "The reason why their son..." Ginzberg, *Legends of the Jews*, vol. 1, p. 515.

CHAPTER 6: MOSES AND PHARAOH

p. 76: "straw is the bond..." Philo of Alexandria, *The Works of Philo*, p. 462.

p. 86: "The darkness was of such..." Ginzberg, *Legends of the Jews*, vol. 1, p. 533.

p. 89: "When they left, they took..." Ginzberg, *Legends of the Jews*, vol. 1, p. 541.

Notes

CHAPTER 7: MIRACLE AT THE RED SEA

p. 92: "The number that pursued..." Josephus, *The New Complete Works of Josephus*, p. 107.

p. 95: "They... seized on the passages..." Josephus, *The New Complete Works of Josephus*, p. 107.

p. 95: "Four centuries of slavery..." Kirsch, *Moses: A Life*, p. 187.

p. 96: "[The sea] was broken and divided..." Philo of Alexandria, The Works of Philo, p. 475.

p. 99: "Showers of rain also came..." Josephus, *The New Complete Works of Josephus*, p. 109.

CHAPTER 8: HARDSHIP IN THE DESERT

p. 100: "With their finger..." Ginzberg, *Legends of the Jews*, vol. 1, p. 560.

p. 100: "The sea cast up..." Ginzberg, *Legends of the Jews*, vol. 1, p. 565–566.

p. 101: "After those many..." Ginzberg, *Legends of the Jews*, vol. 1, p. 569.

p. 102: "Toward evening thick swarms..." Ginzberg, *Legends of the Jews*, vol. 1, p. 573.

p. 102: "had been created on..." Ginzberg, *Legends of the Jews*, vol. 1, p. 570.

p. 102: "throughout forty years..." Ginzberg, *Legends of the Jews*, vol. 1, p. 573.

p. 104: "the most warlike..." Josephus, *The New Complete Works of Josephus*, p. 115.

p. 104: ""Those who try to..." Josephus, *The New Complete Works of Josephus*, p. 115.

p. 106: "Something remarkable but often overlooked..." Kirsch, *Moses: A Life*, p. 226.

p. 107: "Only through the aid..." Ginzberg, *Legends of the Jews*, vol. 1, p. 581.

p. 107: "When they had taken..." Josephus, *The New Complete Works of Josephus*, p. 116.

p. 108: "It strains credulity..." Lawrence E. Stager, "Forging an

134 Moses

p. 112: Identity: The Emergence of Ancient Israel," *The Oxford History of the Biblical World*, ed. Michael Coogan (New York: Oxford University Press, 1998), p. 107.

p. 112: "The forty days . . ." Ginzberg, *Legends of the Jews*, vol. 1, p. 617.

p. 115: "The episode of the . . ." Rabbi Joseph Telushkin, *Jewish Literacy: The Most Important Things to Know about the Jewish Religion, its People, and its History*, rev. ed. (New York: HarperCollins, 2008), p. 44.

CHAPTER 9: HARDSHIP IN THE DESERT

p. 119: "There is hardly . . ." Quoted in Sheler, *Is the Bible True? How Modern Debates and Discoveries Affirm the Essence of the Scriptures*, p. 26.

p. 121: "Whether or not Moses . . ." Quoted in Sheler, *Is the Bible True? How Modern Debates and Discoveries Affirm the Essence of the Scriptures*, p. 27.

p. 123: "At the time when Israel . . ." Ginzberg, *Legends of the Jews*, vol. 1, p. 717.

p. 127: "The slaughter of Midianite women . . ." Kirsch, *Moses: A Life*, p. 323.

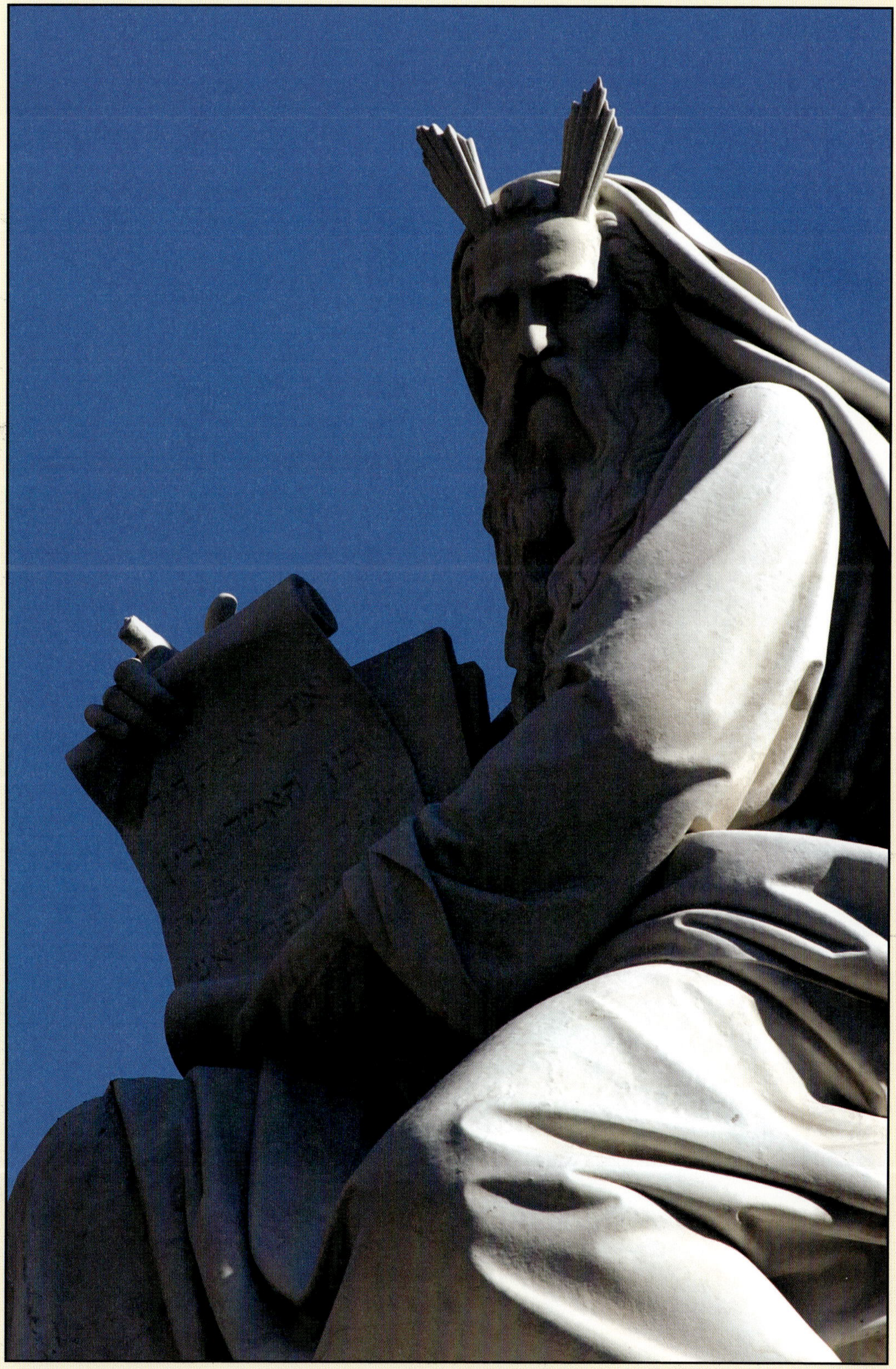

Glossary

Canaan—an ancient region made up of Palestine or the part of it between the Jordan River and the Mediterranean Sea. It is the area of present-day Israel and the West Bank. In the Bible it is the Promised Land of the Israelites.

Haggadah—traditional Jewish literature, especially the nonlegal part of the Talmud.

Hebrew scriptures—the Torah, the Prophets, and the Writings, forming the covenant between God and the Jewish people that is the foundation and Bible of Judaism while constituting for Christians the Old Testament. Also called the Hebrew Bible.

Midrash—any of a group of Jewish commentaries on the Hebrew scriptures compiled between 400 and 1200 CE and based on exegesis, parable, and haggadic legend. The Midrash provided rabbis with an opportunity to explain, expand, and fill in the gaps in the Torah.

pharaoh—a king of ancient Egypt.

Semitic—characteristic of any of a number of peoples of ancient southwestern Asia, including the Hebrews, Arabs, Phoenicians, and Akkadians.

Torah—the first five books of the Hebrew Scriptures (Genesis, Exodus, Leviticus, Numbers, and Deuteronomy), which according to Jewish and Christian tradition were written by Moses.

Further Reading

BOOKS FOR YOUNG READERS

Harris, Geraldine. *Cultural Atlas for Young People: Ancient Egypt* (New York: Facts On File, Inc., 2003).

Hoak, Benjamin. *Joseph*. Philadelphia: Mason Crest, 2009.

Kee, Howard Clark, ed. *The Learning Bible*, Contemporary English Version. New York: American Bible Society, 1995.

Kimmel, Eric A. *Wonders and Miracles, A Passover Companion*. New York, New York: Scholastic Press, 2004.

Wilkinson, Philip. *Eyewitness Christianity*. New York: DK Publishing, Inc., 2006.

BOOKS FOR ADULTS

Armstrong, Karen. *A History of God: The 4,000-Year Quest of Judaism, Christianity, and Islam*. New York: Alfred A. Knopf, 1993.

Coogan, Michael, ed. *The Oxford History of the Biblical World*. New York: Oxford University Press, 1998.

Kirsch, Jonathan. *Moses: A Life*. New York: Ballantine Books, 1998.

Kroll, Woodrow. *Places in the Bible*. Nashville: J. Countryman, 2005.

Sheler, Jeffery L. *Is the Bible True? How Modern Debates and Discoveries Affirm the Essence of the Scriptures*. New York: Harper/Zondervan, 1999.

Sperling, S. David. *The Original Torah: The Political Intent of the Bible's Writers*. New York: New York University Press, 1998.

Internet Resources

http://www.ancientegypt.co.uk/

The British Museum's Web site dedicated to ancient Egypt.

http://www.Bible-history.com

This searchable Web site is a basic Bible encyclopedia, with graphics, maps, pictures and time lines.

http://www.Biblical-art.com

Art and paintings that pertain to Biblical art are featured on this site.

http://www.Jewishencyclopedia.com

The complete contents of the 12-volume Jewish Encyclopedia, originally published 1901–1906, includes much information on Moses.

http://www.sacred-texts.com

The Internet Sacred Text Archive has an enormous repository of electronic texts about religion, mythology, legends and folklore, and occult and esoteric topics. Texts related to Moses include *The Legends of the Jews*, by Louis Ginzberg.

Index

Aaron, 66–67, 89, 106, 117, 122, 124–125
   goes to Pharaoh with Moses, 71–72, 74, 76–79
   and the golden calf, 112–115
Abihu, 122
Abiram, 124
Abraham, 7, 13, 18, 22–23, 37, 53, 60, 68, 104
Ahmose I (Pharaoh), 29, 32
Akki, 43
Amalek, 104, 105
Amalekites, 104–107
Amenhotep II (Pharaoh), 32
Amenhotep IV (Pharaoh), *19*, 32, *75*
Amram, 38, 40, 49, 66
Ark of the Covenant, 112, 117

Baal-Peor (deity), 53, 126
Babylon, 62, 76
Bityah (pharaoh's daughter), 39–40, 42, 46
bricks, 74, 76, 77
burning bush, 59–60, *61*

Caleb, 122, 123, 128
Canaan, 19, 22–24, 25, 31–32, 90, 98, 108, 116, 117, 122–124, 128
circumcision, 67–71
Clines, David J. A., 121
covenant, 22–23, 37, 68, 110, 112, 117

Dathan, 124
deities, *20*, 53, 73–74, 81, 114, 126
Delitzsch, Franz, 27
Deuteronomy (Old Testament book), 6, 8, 12–13, 119, 121
   and the Amalekites, 105
   and Moses's death, 128–129
   and plagues, 82
   See also Old Testament
documentary hypothesis, 119–121, 126

Egypt, 21–22
   deities of, *20*, 73–74, 81
   and genocide, 34, 36–37
   history of, 14–16, 28, 29, 30–37, 48
   Israelites in, 24–29, 28, 31–37, 50–53, 61, 63
   and the New Kingdom, 32, 73, 76, 92–94, 98
   plagues in, 79–89
   plunder of, 6, 63, 89, 100–101
   population of, 98
Eleazar, 125, 128
Eliezer, 70, 107
Esau, 104
Eusebius of Caesarea, 31, 40
Exodus (Old Testament book), 16–17, 27, 119–121
   and the Amalekites, 106
   and brick-making, 74, 77

Numbers in ***bold italics*** refer to captions.

140 *Moses*

and the burning bush, 59–60
and circumcision, 67–69
and coal test, 43–44
and covenant with God, 37
dates of events in, 29, 30
and the freeing of the Israelites, 63, 65–66, 67, 74, 76, 77–78
and God's anger with Moses, 71
and idol worship, 113, 114–115
and Israelites in the desert, 90, 92, 101–102, 104, 109
and the Israelites' plunder of Egypt, 6, 63
and Israelities in Egypt, 29, 33, 34, 36
and Jethro, 108–109
manna, 102–103
and Moses as author of the Pentateuch, 118–119
and Moses in Midian, 54
and Moses in the Nile River, 39–40
Moses kills an Egyptian overseer, 51
Moses learns his ancestry, 50
Moses's birth, 38
and Moses's miracles, 64, 72
and Moses's son, 57
and Mount Sinai, 110
and the name of God, 61, 62
and plagues in Egypt, 79–89
and population of Israelites, 98
and the Red Sea, 99
and the Ten Commandments, 111, 112, 117
and the Tent of Meeting (tabernacle), 117
and Zipporah, 71
See also Old Testament

famine, 21–22
folktales. *See* legends
Friedman, Richard Elliott, 17, 119

Gabriel (angel), 43–44
Genesis (Old Testament book), 7–8, 22–24, 119–121
and circumcision, 68

and Israelites in Egypt, 26, 29
and Joseph, 25, 27, 89
See also Old Testament
Gershom, 57, 70
Gesenius, Wilhelm, 62
Ginzberg, Louis, 13, 42, 44, 56, 112
God. *See* Yahweh
Goshen, 27, 28–29, 31, 33, 38, *82*, 85
See also Egypt
Gregory of Nyssa, 49–50, 55

Habiru, 18–20
See also Israelites
Heber. *See* Moses
Heliopolis, 33, 45
Herodotus, 21
Hobab. *See* Jethro
Horus, *20*, 73–74
Hur, 106, 112–113
Hyksos, 28, 29, 32, 92

idol worship, 113–115, 126
Irenaeus, 48
Isaac, 8, *23*, 37, 60, 104
Isis, 73–74
Israelites
and the Amalekites, 104–107
complaints of, to Moses, 95–96, 101–104
in the desert, 90–92, 101–104, 109
in Egypt, 24–29, 28, 31–37, 50–53, 61, 63
God's promise to free the, 63
and idol worship, 113–115, 126
and the Midianites, 108–109, 126–128
and oral history, 16, 108–109
origins of the, 22–24
and plunder of the Egyptians, 6, 63, 89, 100–101
population of, 98
and the Red Sea, 95–97, 99
revolts of, against Moses, 122–125
See also Moses

Jacob, 8, 23–24, 25–26, 37, 60, 104
Jekuthiel. *See* Moses

Jesus Christ, 7, 9, 56, 119
Jethro, 54–55, *57*, 58, 67, 70,
    107–109
Jewish Antiquities (Josephus), 40, 48,
    92, 99, 105
Jewish Encyclopedia, 66–67
Jochebed, 38–40, 49, 66
Joseph, 8, 24, 26–28, 29, 89
Josephus, Flavius, 17, 32, 40, 44, 48,
    51–52, 92, 95
    and the Amalekites, 104–105, 106,
        107
    and Moses in Midian, 55
    and Moses's exile from Egypt, 53
    and the Red Sea, 99
Joshua, 106–107, 115, 122, 128

Keil, Carl Friedrich, 27
Kirsch, Jonathan, 95, 106, 127
Korah, 124

legends, 8, 40
    Mesopotamian, 43
    midrashim, 17, 34, 37, 50, 56, 58,
        70, 85–86, 96, 101–102, 113,
        123
    and Moses's childhood, 42–44,
        46–47
    and Moses's speech impediment,
        65
    and Moses's wealth, 6, 11
    and plunder of Egyptian bodies,
        100–101
Legends of the Jews (Ginzberg), 13,
    50, 56, 85, 89
Levites, 49, 67, 115

Manetho, 45
manna, 102–103
Merneptah, 31–32
Merris. *See* Bityah (pharaoh's daughter)
Midian, 53–55, 57–60, 71, 85–86,
    107–109, 126–128
midrashim, 17, 34, 37, 50, 56, 58,
    70, 96, 101–102, 113, 123
    See also legends
Miriam, 39–40, 66, 106, 122, 124

Moody, Dwight L., *16*
Moses
    adoption of, 6
    and the Amalekites, 105
    as author of the Pentateuch, 12,
        118–119, 121
    birth of, 38–39
    and the burning bush, 59–60, *61*
    childhood of, 42–44
    children of, 57, 67, 70, 107
    and circumcision, 67–71
    death of, 128–129
    depictions of, with horns, *116*
    education of, 44–47
    and freeing the Israelites, 63,
        65–67, 74–79, 89
    and Gabriel's test, 43–44
    and Israelites' complaints, 95–96,
        101–104
    kills Egyptian overseer, 51–52
    learns his ancestry, 49–50
    marriage of, to Zipporah, 55, 57,
        67, 70–71, 107
    in Midian, 53–55, 57–60
    miracles of, 63–65, 72, 104, 125
    name of, 16–17, 40–42
    and the name of God, 60–63
    and the Nile River, 39–40, *41*, 43
    and plagues of Egypt, 79–89
    as real person, 13–14, 16–17, 129
    and revolts, 122–125
    as shepherd, 55, 56, 57–60
    as soldier, 48
    and the Ten Commandments, 6,
        10, 12, 110–113, 115–117
    wealth of, 6, 11–12, *113*, 129
    See also Aaron; Israelites
Moses: A Life (Kirsch), 95, 106, 127
Moses: A Man of Selfless Dedication
    (Swindoll), 68
Mount Horeb, 59
Mount Sinai, *10*, 110, *111*, 112, 114,
    116, 122

Nadab, 122
New Kingdom, 32, 73, 76, 92–94, 98
    See also Egypt
New Testament, 7, 9, 13, 44–45, 47,

51, 56, 119
Nile River, 6, 21, 39, *41*, 43
   as blood, 79, *81*, 87
Numbers (Old Testament book), 121, 122–124, 125, 126, 127, 128
   See also Old Testament

Old Testament, 7, 8, 9, 54, 56, 65, 108, 118, 119, 121–123
   and authorship, 12, 118–121
   and circumcision, 69–71
   dates of events in, 29–30
   See also Exodus (Old Testament book); Genesis (Old Testament book)
Old Testament History (Pfeiffer), 28, 46
On (Heliopolis), 33, 45
Osiris, 73–74
The Oxford History of the Biblical World (Stager), 108–109

Passover, *35*, 87–88
Pentateuch, 12, 118, 121
   See also Old Testament
Pfeiffer, Charles F., 28, 46, 69
pharaohs, 15, 27–29, 31–33, 36–37, 42–44, 74–86, 89, 92–95, 99
   See also Egypt
pharaoh's daughter. *See* Bityah (pharaoh's daughter)
Philo of Alexandria, 17, 51, 52, 56, 76
   and enslavement of Israelities, 34
   and Moses's education, 47
   and the Red Sea, 96, 99
pillars of fire and clouds, 91, 96
plagues, 79–89
population, 98

Ramesses II. *See* Ramses II (Pharaoh)
Ramses II (Pharaoh), 15, 18, 30–31, 33, 73
Ras es-Safsaf. *See* Mount Horeb
Red Sea, 53, 94, 95–97, 99
Rephidim, 103–104, 105, 106
Reuel. *See* Jethro

Sargon, 43
Sea of Reeds, 94
   See also Red Sea
Septuagint, 33, 42
Seth, 73–74
shepherds, 26–28, 53–55, 56
Sinuhe, 46
Song of Miriam, 99
Song of Moses, 99
Stager, Lawrence E., 108–109
Stephen, 44–45, 48
Stoic philosophy, 47
Succoth, 89, 91
Swindoll, Charles, 68

Talmud, 56
Telushkin, Joseph, 115–116
Ten Commandments, 6, *10*, 12, 110–113, 115–117
Tent of Meeting, 117, 123
Thermuthis. *See* Bityah (pharaoh's daughter)
Thutmose III (Pharaoh), 30
Tobia. *See* Moses
Torah, 12, 111–112, 118
   See also Old Testament

Ussher, James, 30

wealth
   and faith, 7–9
   of Moses, 6, 11–12, *113*, 129
Wellhausen, Julius, 120
Who Wrote the Bible (Friedman), 17

Yahweh, 60–63, 90, 92, 99
   anger of, with Israelites, 114–115, 126–127
   anger of, with Moses, 71
   Jethro's worship of, 107–108
   as pillar of cloud, 91, 96
   as pillar of fire, 91, 96
   and the Ten Commandments, 110, 112, 116–117

Zipporah, 55, 57, 67, 70–71, 107
Zoser (Pharaoh), 21–22

Illustration Credits

2:	used under license from Shutterstock, Inc.	75:	The Jewish Museum, New York/Art Resource, NY
10:	Scala/Ministero per i Beni e le Attavità culturali/Art Resource, NY	78:	Erich Lessing/Art Resource, NY
15:	used under license from Shutterstock, Inc.	81:	used under license from Shutterstock, Inc.
16:	© 2009 Jupiterimages Corporation	82:	used under license from Shutterstock, Inc.
19:	© the Trustees of the British Museum/Art Resource, NY	84:	Victoria & Albert Museum, London/Art Resource, NY
20:	used under license from Shutterstock, Inc.	88:	used under license from Shutterstock, Inc.
23:	© 2009 Jupiterimages Corporation	91:	The Tate Gallery, London/Art Resource, NY
26:	Erich Lessing/Art Resource, NY		
31:	© 2009 Jupiterimages Corporation	93:	used under license from Shutterstock, Inc.
35:	Erich Lessing/Art Resource, NY		
36:	used under license from Shutterstock, Inc.	97:	© 2009 Jupiterimages Corporation
		103:	Scala/Ministero per i Beni e le Attavità culturali/Art Resource, NY
41:	Réunion des Musées Nationaux/Art Resource, NY	111:	used under license from Shutterstock, Inc.
44:	Réunion des Musées Nationaux/Art Resource, NY	113:	used under license from Shutterstock, Inc.
51:	The Jewish Museum, New York/Art Resource, NY	114:	Erich Lessing/Art Resource, NY
		116:	used under license from Shutterstock, Inc.
54:	Réunion des Musées Nationaux/Art Resource, NY	120:	used under license from Shutterstock, Inc.
56:	© 2009 Jupiterimages Corporation		
57:	Scala/Art Resource, NY	125:	© 2009 Jupiterimages Corporation
61:	Réunion des Musées Nationaux/Art Resource, NY	135:	used under license from Shutterstock, Inc.
69	Scala/Art Resource, NY		

Cover photo: "Moses and the Tablets of the Law" by Laurent de La Hire or La Hyre (1606-56). Private collection/Bonhams, London, UK/ The Bridgeman Art Library

DOROTHY KAVANAUGH is the author of several books, including Islam, Christianity, and Judaism (Mason Crest, 2004). A graduate of Bryn Mawr College, she lives with her family in the suburbs of Philadelphia.